THE MANDELBROT AND JULIA SETS

A Tool Kit of Dynamics Activities

ROBERT L. DEVANEY

KEY CURRICULUM PRESS
Innovators in Mathematics Education

Editor	Casey FitzSimons
Project Administrator	James A. Browne
Production Editors	Jason Luz, Jennifer Strada
Copy Editor	Margaret Moore
Production and Manufacturing Manager	Diana Jean Parks
Production Coordinator	Ann Rothenbuhler
Text and Cover Designer	Kirk Mills
Compositor	Jenny K. Somerville
Technical Artists	Ben Turner Graphics
Art and Design Coordinator	Caroline Ayres
Prepress	TSI Graphics
Printer	Versa Press, Inc.
Publisher	Steven Rasmussen

This material is based upon work supported by the National Science Foundation under award number ESI-9255724. Any opinions, findings, and conclusions or recommendations expressed in this publication are those of the author and do not necessarily reflect the views of the National Science Foundation.

Key Curriculum Press
1150 65th Street
Emeryville, CA 94608
510-595-7000
editorial@keypress.com
http://www.keypress.com

Printed in the United States of America   10 9 8 7 6 5 4 3 2 1   03 02 01 00 99   ISBN 1-55953-357-9

CONTENTS

Curriculum Correlation Key

◗	Small portion of lesson is relevant to indicated stage of curriculum.	MS	Middle School
◑	About half of lesson is relevant.	A1	Algebra
●	Entire lesson is relevant.	G	Geometry
		A2	Algebra 2
◉	Lesson is particularly relevant and could replace a traditional lesson.	P/C	Precalculus or Calculus

THE MANDELBROT AND JULIA SETS: A TOOL KIT OF DYNAMICS ACTIVITIES

©2000 KEY CURRICULUM PRESS

Letter from the Author

Dear Educator,

Welcome to *The Mandelbrot and Julia Sets: A Tool Kit of Dynamics Activities*, the fourth in our collection of workbooks designed to introduce students to the marvelous new area of mathematics called dynamical systems. From the first day we began to expose our students to these contemporary ideas, we have been committed to helping others spark interest in their students by exposing them to the beauty and mystery of these rich mathematical topics. In assembling this book, we have attempted to provide you with a blend of explanations, investigations, and teacher information to facilitate your journey into this relatively unexplored new world!

This is by no means a typical mathematics textbook. Rather, it is a stepping stone to allow students to investigate mathematical ideas in a way that is very different from their usual classroom experiences. Many students have seen images of the Mandelbrot set and the Julia sets. Some may have written computer programs to draw these pictures. However, few realize the beautiful and accessible mathematics that lies behind these images. Our goal in this book is to make at least some of these ideas available to students and teachers alike.

We realize that much of this material is unfamiliar to teachers, having been developed after many of today's teachers finished their schooling. This presents both a wonderful and daunting opportunity for teachers. How do we expose our students to what is new and exciting in mathematics if we don't understand all of it ourselves? What has worked well for us is to let the students plunge forward independently. Let them read and think and discover on their own. If they have questions, open the discussion up to all. Everyone, including the teacher, learns in this way. If you reach an impasse where nobody seems to know the answer, so what! Leave that hole unfilled and move on. This is the way research in mathematics is always done. Every once in a while someone in the class will have a little insight. When that happens, it is often the magical moment when everything finally fits together and everyone learns.

Curriculum Links

Although this book can be used as a stand-alone supplementary unit in many mathematics courses, its real strength lies in integrating it within the existing secondary school mathematics curriculum by treating it as a contemporary strand in mathematics. Many of the topics covered in this book mesh very nicely with topics in algebra courses, and the use of technology is an essential feature of this topic. For example, all of the main ideas in the book involve the algebra and geometry of complex numbers. In Lesson 3 we make essential use of both of these facets when we describe the Julia set for the (complex) squaring rule. Beyond this special example, computation of the Mandelbrot and Julia sets demands access to high level computers.

The Contents pages contain icons that help you identify how specific lessons correlate with different points in the traditional curriculum.

Lesson Contents

At the beginning of each lesson you will find a set of *Teacher Notes.* These notes begin with a short *Overview* of the lesson, which briefly describes the main focus of the lesson. Next we discuss the *Mathematical Prerequisites* and *Mathematical Connections* for this lesson. It is important to note that even though a mathematical topic is listed as a prerequisite, it may in fact be a corequisite, meaning that it can be taught along with the lesson if students have not been exposed to it beforehand.

Technology options are also described to help you make the best use of the technology available to you. In many situations, you will have to use the computer to present the material. You simply cannot iterate a given function enough times by hand in order to compute the Julia or Mandelbrot set. There are several Java applets available at the Dynamical Systems and Technology Web site **http://math.bu.edu/DYSYS** that were developed specifically for this workbook. These applets run on any computing platform and may be downloaded from this Web site free of charge. Be sure to check out the Mandelbrot Set Explorer at that Web site as well. Unlike most software packages, the Explorer consists of a series of stored pictures that you can download at will; you do not need to spend time computing these images.

The video called *The Fractal Geometry of the Mandelbrot Set* is a 70-minute animated overview of many of the subjects of this text. We suggest that you share this video with your students in conjunction with Lessons 4–6 in this book.

Each section of the book is organized as follows. The *Suggested Lesson Plan* section describes the amount of time needed, possible organizational and presentation strategies, and suggested homework assignments. Keep in mind that these are only suggestions; your own teaching situation may dictate a different structure of time allocation. The *Lesson Notes* contain an assortment of suggestions, ideas, and possible extensions connected with the material in the section.

The **Explanation** pages introduce the mathematical content of the lesson and are intended for you or your students to read. You may want to photocopy the pages for your students, or you may prefer to summarize the concepts using transparencies. In some cases, the material is ideal for student experimentation and individual discovery.

The **Investigations** that follow are in blackline-master format, allowing students to record their answers directly on a photocopy of each page. These are ideal for students to work through cooperatively.

Finally, the back of the book contains a thorough and detailed answer to every problem.

Acknowledgments

As with any project that evolves over time, we have many people to thank for their encouragement and assistance. This book grew out of a five-year project sponsored by the National Science Foundation. We are particularly indebted to James Sandefur and Spud Bradley for their support during this period. Many teachers participated in the four-year series of summer workshops that helped to define these materials. We are most appreciative of the work of the lead teachers in these efforts: Beverly Mawn, Jamil Siddiqui, Rob Quaden, Liz Perry, John Bookston, Al Coons, Kathy Leggat, Megan Staples, Jim Carpenter, and Gerald Nimetz. Eileen Lee contributed enormously to the project in the early stages by refining and elaborating on our original notes. Masha Albrecht also contributed a number of fine ideas regarding the organization of these notes. Numerous people contributed to the technology portion of this project, including Clara Bodelon, Rodin Enchev, Noah Goodmann, Kevin Lee, Alex Kasman, Adrian Vajiac, and Johanna Voolich. It is also a pleasure to thank the folks at Key Curriculum Press, especially Steve Rasmussen and David Rasmussen, Jason Luz, James Browne, and Casey FitzSimons for their enthusiasm and helpfulness in bringing this project to a successful conclusion. Finally, we are deeply indebted to Jonathan Choate and Alice Foster, who worked with us for many long hours in the initial stages of this project, trying desperately to keep the mathematical ideas in this book at an appropriate level.

We hope that you find these materials helpful and the mathematical content exciting, stimulating, and challenging. We welcome any comments and/or suggestions about this project. We can be reached via the Web site above.

Robert L. Devaney

RELATED WEB SITE

Check out the Dynamical Systems and Technology Web site at
http://math.bu.edu/DYSYS for free downloadable Java applets
relevant to this book.

A Note To Students

Dear Student,

Welcome to the fourth and final book in *A Tool Kit of Dynamics Activities* series. This book will be very different from previous books in this series in that almost all the mathematical ideas that we will touch on have been discovered within the past 20 years. Indeed, there are some topics we will discuss that have been discovered only in the past 5 years.

As a consequence, unlike most mathematical topics that you have learned in school, we will not be able to present all of this material in complete detail. In fact, some of the ideas in this book are understood completely by only a handful of research mathematicians. Nevertheless, we will try to give you at least a taste of some of this mathematics.

Another way this book differs from others in the series is that you definitely need to have some computer software to do the Investigations. Graphing calculators are not powerful enough at this time to handle the millions of computations necessary to investigate the Mandelbrot and Julia sets. Luckily plenty of free software is available on the Internet. We urge you to check out the Dynamical Systems and Technology Web site **http://math.bu.edu/DYSYS** to find pointers to available software that you can use to perform these experiments. There are a number of Java applets available at this site that are relevant to this series. We urge you to familiarize yourself with these tools.

The video called *The Fractal Geometry of the Mandelbrot Set* is a 70-minute animated overview of many of the subjects of this text. We suggest that you watch this video in conjunction with Lessons 4–6 in this book.

As for mathematical prerequisites for reading this book, you must be familiar with complex numbers and the geometry of the complex plane, as well as with concepts from algebra (graphing, solving quadratic equations, and so forth). Some of the ideas in previous books in this series will be helpful as you read this book, but you do not need to be familiar with all the topics in these books in order to read this one. We will begin with a review of iteration (orbits, fixed points, cycles, and so forth). These are the main prerequisites from the earlier material.

We do not expect you to understand everything you read in this book. While the entire book deals with quadratic expressions of the form $x^2 + c$, when iterated, these simple quadratic expressions lead to incredibly complicated mathematical ideas and geometric shapes. That is the beauty of the subject!

You certainly will not be able to prove the things we describe. Don't be surprised if the mathematics teachers in your school cannot answer your questions about this material. For many questions, nobody knows the answer! You may be the first person to formulate certain questions! Maybe you will even be the first person to be able to answer these questions! If so, you will have experienced one of the thrills of doing mathematical research.

So, good luck! Fasten your seat belt for a wild ride through some of the most exciting mathematics around! Feel free to send e-mail to me if you have questions: I cannot guarantee that I will have the time to or even be able to answer the questions asked, but I will try.

Professor Robert L. Devaney

Department of Mathematics
Boston University
e-mail: bob@bu.edu

A Little History

The history of the Mandelbrot and Julia sets is on the one hand brief, and on the other hand, ongoing. In the late nineteenth century, mathematicians were interested in understanding a process called "linearization." Basically, this means taking an intractable problem and approximating it by one that is solvable. The natural question is: How good is the approximation? Or what are the conditions under which the approximation breaks down?

These are the questions that led two French mathematicians, Gaston Julia (1892–1978) and Pierre Fatou (1878–1929), to investigate iteration of complex functions during the period 1918–1920. They discovered that the set of places where the approximation breaks down is a very complicated subset of the complex plane. This is the set that we now call the Julia set. Amazingly, without the aid of a computer, these mathematicians could "see" these complicated shapes, if only in their minds. Although they were working with the iteration rule $x \rightarrow x^2 + c$, much as we will do in this book, they never thought to draw the quintessential picture associated with this rule, the Mandelbrot set.

In very short order, Julia and Fatou reached insurmountable mathematical difficulties; they could not eliminate such possibilities as "wandering domains." Also, because Julia and Fatou had no access to computers and computer graphics and could not share the beauty that they were seeing with others, the study of complex dynamics (as the field is now known) died out in the early 1920s.

This changed dramatically in 1980, when Benoit Mandelbrot (1924–) discovered the incredibly intricate image that now bears his name. Mandelbrot at that time was a researcher at IBM and thus had access to some of the most powerful computers of the time. He made conjectures about the images he was seeing and showed the computer graphics to numerous mathematicians. A number of eminent mathematicians immediately began to study these objects with tools (both mathematical and computational) that Julia and Fatou never had access to. Adrien Douady (Paris) and John Hubbard (Cornell University) made great inroads into understanding the geometry of the Mandelbrot set. Later they were joined by Bodil Branner (Copenhagen), who showed them how her studies of cubic polynomials complemented those of quadratics. Dennis Sullivan (City University of New York) made one of the fundamental discoveries, the so-called "No Wandering Domains" theorem, that successfully eliminated the impasse reached by Julia and Fatou. Several younger mathematicians, Jean-Christophe Yoccoz (Paris) and Curt McMullen (Harvard

University), were awarded the Fields' Medal in 1994 and 1998, respectively, for their pioneering studies of the Mandelbrot and Julia sets. And most of this work deals only with that simple quadratic iteration rule.

When one considers other complex iteration rules, the situation becomes much more difficult. For one thing, the analogue of the Mandelbrot set for cubics lies in four-dimensional space, not the plane. This makes visualization and geometry much more difficult. My students and I have spent the last twenty years trying to understand the dynamics of the (complex) sine, cosine, and exponential functions. Progress has been made, but a lot more remains to be done. That's the nature of mathematical research: One problem and its solution often leads to many, many more interesting and unsolved problems.

Quadratic Iteration

OVERVIEW

This lesson is a review of quadratic iteration. Students who have studied the third book of this series, *Chaos,* will find that this lesson is a review of material presented in that book. In particular, many of the Investigations in the final lesson of *Chaos* relate to the material discussed here.

MATHEMATICAL PREREQUISITES

Students need to be familiar with the basics of iteration including orbits, fixed points, and cycles, especially attracting fixed points and cycles, in order to understand the remainder of this book. In this lesson we quickly review these ideas. We also review two ways to visualize orbits: time series and graphical iteration. Strictly speaking, these images are not necessary for the remainder of the book, since these pictures are not relevant for iterations in the complex plane. Nevertheless, they are quite useful to understand the fate of orbits of the iteration rule $x \rightarrow x^2 + c$ when c is a real number.

MATHEMATICAL CONNECTIONS

Graphing of functions and **solving equations,** especially quadratic equations, are important in this lesson. The concept of **iteration** is crucial throughout the book.

TECHNOLOGY

You may iterate expressions on most contemporary calculators by simply depressing a key repeatedly. Also, spreadsheets are an effective way of computing orbits of $x \rightarrow x^2 + c$ and then varying the parameter c to witness the changes. For graphical iteration, many graphing calculators (such as the TI-83) have the facility to draw web diagrams. You may also use the Java applet titled "Nonlinear Web" at **http://math.bu.edu/DYSYS/applets** to iterate graphically.

SUGGESTED LESSON PLAN

CLASS TIME

For students who have covered some of the *Chaos* book in this series, this lesson can serve mainly as review material. One 50-minute class period should be sufficient to review the relevant material.

PREPARATION

Read through the Explanation, paying particular attention to the section "The critical orbit." We will see later that it is the orbit of 0 (the critical orbit) that plays a . . . errh . . . critical role in determining the Mandelbrot set. In particular, later we will be very concerned with the question: When does the critical orbit escape?

LESSON DEVELOPMENT

First review iteration and then have students complete Investigation 1. They should be able to make statements like "Orbit tends to a fixed point" or "Orbit tends to a 2-cycle" or "Orbit tends to infinity" without difficulty. A calculator or spreadsheet is most useful for this activity.

The section on time series can safely be skipped. It is simply a way for students to visualize orbits, often the easiest way of detecting cycles or other fates of orbits. However, make sure to cover the material in the section "The critical orbit." If students are familiar with graphical iteration, you can use that to illustrate that the critical orbit tends to infinity when $c > 0.25$ and when $c < -2$. Use Transparencies 1A and 1B for this purpose. The box in Transparency 1A is there only to guide you as you perform the graphical iteration; it is not part of the web diagram. Students should see that the critical orbit escapes to infinity since the web diagram moves outside this box and never returns.

Graphical iteration is used very rarely in the coming lessons. We include it here primarily as a tool for use in Investigation 3. Have students complete Investigation 2 to help them recall the process of graphical iteration. Then they can turn their attention to Investigation 3, where they will look for points that do or do not escape to infinity under iteration of $x \rightarrow x^2 + c$ when $c < -2$. The goal is to have students understand that this non-escape set breaks up into lots of intervals. We will see this again later when we investigate filled Julia sets that disintegrate into fractal dust. Of course, students do not have that terminology yet, but this is a lead-in to what will be covered later.

LESSON NOTES

The material on attracting and repelling fixed points is optional and can be used primarily for review. In the coming lessons we will often say, "Orbits are attracted to a cycle of period n." It is important that students know what this sentence means. However, they need not know in detail what attracting and repelling fixed points and cycles are in order to understand this statement. The examples in Investigation 1 (and in Lesson 2: Complex Linear Iteration) should be sufficient for this purpose.

Finding the cycles of period 2 (Investigation 6) using division of polynomials is a worthwhile review for students who have a solid background in algebra, but it is not essential for the subsequent material. Similarly, Investigations 4 and 5 are optional.

$$x \rightarrow x^2 - 2.2$$

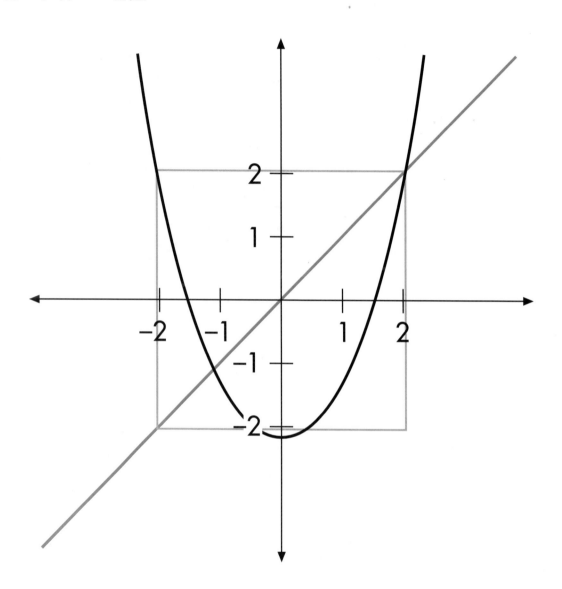

$$x \rightarrow x^2 + 0.5$$

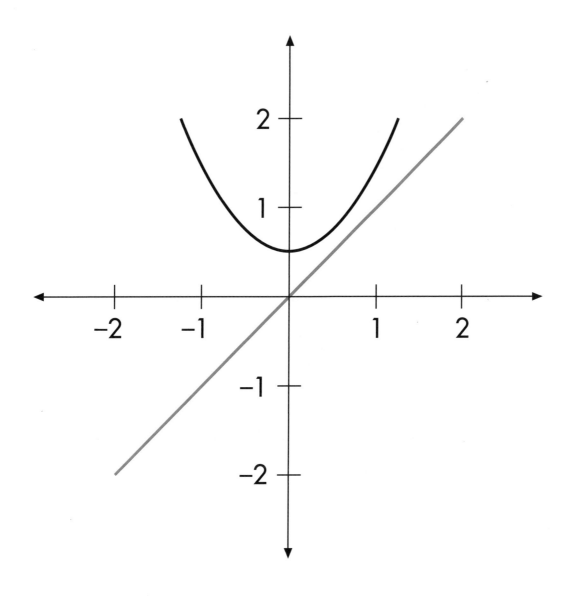

In this book, we will concentrate on iterations involving complex numbers and complex quadratic iteration rules. Before we do that, we need to spend some time recalling some of the remarkable things that happen when we iterate real quadratic polynomials. In this lesson, let's investigate the iteration rule $x \rightarrow x^2 + c$ where both x and c are real numbers. The number c is called a **parameter**. For each different choice of the parameter, we get a different iteration rule.

FATES OF ORBITS

As you have seen in the book *Chaos* in this series, the **fate** of orbits of quadratic iteration rules depends on both the **seed** and the particular choice of the parameter. For example, for $c = 1$ the iteration rule is $x \rightarrow x^2 + 1$. The **orbit** of 0 tends to infinity:

$$0 \rightarrow 1 \rightarrow 2 \rightarrow 5 \rightarrow 26 \rightarrow 677 \rightarrow \cdots$$

When you let $c = 0$, a very different fate occurs. The orbit remains fixed at 0:

$$0 \rightarrow 0 \rightarrow 0 \rightarrow 0 \rightarrow 0 \rightarrow \cdots$$

When $c = -1$, we find another fate. The orbit cycles with period 2:

$$0 \rightarrow -1 \rightarrow 0 \rightarrow -1 \rightarrow 0 \rightarrow -1 \rightarrow \cdots$$

When $c = -2$, the orbit of 0 is eventually **fixed:**

$$0 \rightarrow -2 \rightarrow 2 \rightarrow 2 \rightarrow 2 \rightarrow 2 \rightarrow \cdots$$

But if you keep the same parameter ($c = -2$) and change the seed to $x_0 = 0.1$, the orbit has a very different fate. Here is a list of the first 30 points on this orbit:

Iteration	Orbit
0	0.1
1	−1.99
2	1.9601
3	1.841992
4	1.392935
5	−0.05973
6	−1.99643
7	1.98574
8	1.943165
9	1.775891
10	1.153789

Iteration	Orbit
11	−0.66877
12	−1.55274
13	0.411015
14	−1.83107
15	1.352805
16	−0.16992
17	−1.97113
18	1.885343
19	1.554517
20	0.416525
21	−1.82651

Iteration	Orbit
22	1.336129
23	−0.21476
24	−1.95388
25	1.81764
26	1.303816
27	−0.30006
28	−1.90996
29	1.647951
30	0.715743

As you have seen before, this iteration rule leads to orbits that **depend sensitively on initial conditions.**

VISUALIZING ORBITS

It is often helpful to visualize orbits as pictures rather than as long lists of numbers. There are several ways to do this. In a **time-series graph**, we plot the iteration count $(0, 1, 2, \ldots)$ on the horizontal axis and the numerical values of the orbit vertically. For example, the time-series plot corresponding to the orbit of 0 for the iteration rule $x \rightarrow x^2 - 1$ is

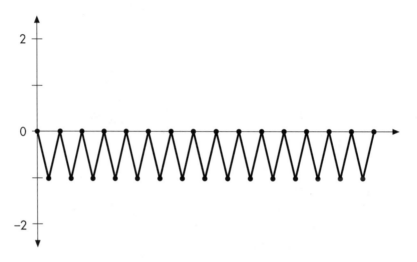

Similarly, if we plot the time series for the iteration rule $x \rightarrow x^2 - 2$ using the seed $x_0 = 0.1$, we find

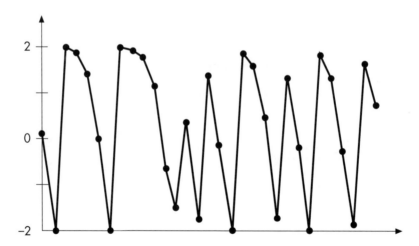

a very different time-series plot indeed!

GRAPHICAL ITERATION

Another way to visualize orbits of the iteration rule $x \rightarrow x^2 + c$ is to use **graphical iteration.** To do this, we plot the graphs of both $y = x^2 + c$ and the diagonal line $y = x$ on the same graph. To display the orbit of the seed x_0, we begin on the diagonal line $y = x$ just above x_0 at the point (x_0, x_0). Then we draw a vertical line to the graph of $y = x^2 + c$ followed by a horizontal line to the diagonal $y = x$. We reach the diagonal at the point (x_1, x_1), directly over the next point on the orbit, namely, x_1. Then we repeat this process, starting at (x_1, x_1) and ending at (x_2, x_2). Eventually we see the orbit displayed as a collection of junction points along the diagonal. For example, graphical iteration of the rule $x \rightarrow x^2 + 0.5$ shows that the orbit of x_0 goes to infinity:

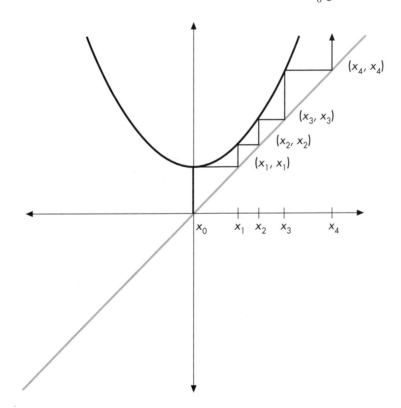

When we consider instead the iteration rule $x \rightarrow x^2 - 0.9$, we see that some orbits tend to a **2-cycle** at

$$-0.88 \ldots \rightarrow -0.11 \ldots \rightarrow -0.88 \ldots \rightarrow -0.11 \ldots$$

In the first figure we plot the orbit of −0.4, which tends to the 2-cycle. Next to it we plot just the orbit of the 2-cycle:

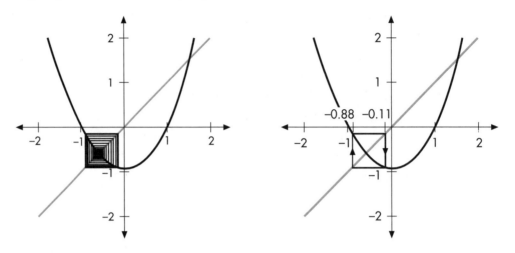

And when the iteration rule is $x \to x^2 - 2$ with seed $x_0 = 0.1$, we see **chaotic behavior:**

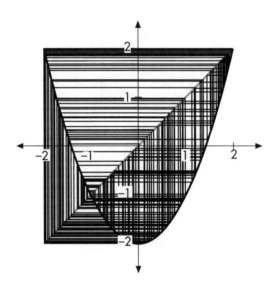

THE CRITICAL ORBIT

When you begin to investigate the Mandelbrot set, it will be the orbit of the seed 0 that will be most important. The orbit of 0 is called the **critical point** of the iteration rule $x \to x^2 + c$ and the orbit of 0 is the **critical orbit.** The reason that 0 is so special is that the minimum value of the graph of $y \to x^2 + c$ occurs when $x = 0$. (For students who know some calculus, this means that the derivative of $x^2 + c$ vanishes at 0. Places where the derivative is 0 play a special role in determining much of the mathematical behavior of an expression such as $x^2 + c$.)

An important issue for us will be: When does the critical orbit tend to infinity? That is, when does the critical orbit "escape"? To answer this for real values of the parameter c, we can resort to graphical iteration. For if the graph of $y = x^2 + c$ always lies above the diagonal $y = x$, then all orbits (not just the critical orbit) tend to infinity:

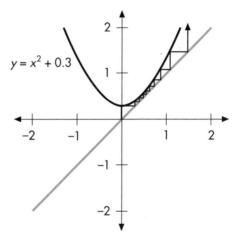

$$y = x^2 + 0.3$$

To find the c-values for which the graph lies above the diagonal, we can simply find the c-values for which the iteration rule $x \to x^2 + c$ has no fixed points. So we solve $x^2 + c = x$ or $x^2 - x + c = 0$.

By the quadratic formula, the roots of this equation are

$$p_\pm = \frac{1 \pm \sqrt{1 - 4c}}{2}$$

So we have two roots if $c < \frac{1}{4}$, just one root if $c = \frac{1}{4}$, and no roots if $c > \frac{1}{4}$. Thus, the graph of $y = x^2 + c$ lies above the diagonal when $c > \frac{1}{4}$ and so the critical orbit escapes. Indeed, all orbits escape.

There is another way the critical orbit can escape. Look at the fixed point that we called p_+. This fixed point is always positive since

$$p_+ = \frac{1 + \sqrt{1 - 4c}}{2} > 0$$

as long as $c \leq \frac{1}{4}$. Now look at the graph of $y = x^2 + c$. We superimpose a square on this graph with vertices at (p_+, p_+) and $(-p_+, -p_+)$. It is important to remember that this square is **not** a picture of graphical iteration.

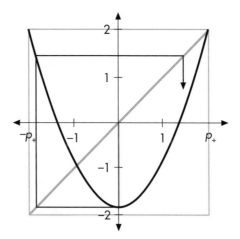

Notice that the orbit of 0 is constrained to lie within this box provided that $y = 0^2 + c = c \geq -p_+$.

If $y = 0^2 + c = c < -p_+$, then the graph of $y = x^2 + c$ pokes out through the bottom of the box and the critical orbit escapes to infinity:

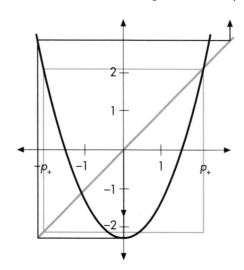

THE MANDELBROT AND JULIA SETS: A TOOL KIT OF DYNAMICS ACTIVITIES
©2000 KEY CURRICULUM PRESS

To find the c-values where this happens, we need to find those c's for which

$$c < -p_+ = -\frac{1 + \sqrt{1 - 4c}}{2}$$

This happens when

$$2c + 1 < -\sqrt{1 - 4c} < 0$$

or when we square both sides. (Remember, both sides of this inequality are negative before we square, so the inequality sign is reversed!)

$$4c^2 + 4c + 1 > 1 - 4c$$

$$\text{or } 4c^2 + 8c > 0$$

This happens when $c > 0$ (which is not the case we are interested in) and also when $c < -2$. So when $c < -2$, the graph of $y = x^2 + c$ pokes through the bottom of the box and the critical orbit escapes.

To summarize, we see that for the iteration rule $x \to x^2 + c$ the critical orbit escapes when $c > \frac{1}{4}$ or $c < -2$.

FIXED POINTS

There are several different varieties of fixed points. The type of fixed point is determined by the behavior of nearby orbits. **Attracting fixed points** have the property that nearby orbits tend to the fixed point. **Repelling fixed points** have the property that nearby orbits move away from the fixed point. Orbits of points near a repelling fixed point may eventually return close to the fixed point, but initially must move away. **Neutral fixed points** are neither atttracting nor repelling.

ATTRACTING AND REPELLING FIXED POINTS

Finding fixed points is relatively easy. We can solve the equation $x^2 + c = x$ for a given c-value, or we can look for places where the graph of $y = x^2 + c$ crosses the diagonal $y = x$. To determine whether a fixed point is attracting or repelling, we must examine the position of the graph of $y = x^2 + c$ relative to the diagonal. If the graph crosses the diagonal with a slope greater than 1, then the fixed point must be repelling. But if the slope of the graph at the fixed point is between 0 and 1, then the fixed point is attracting.

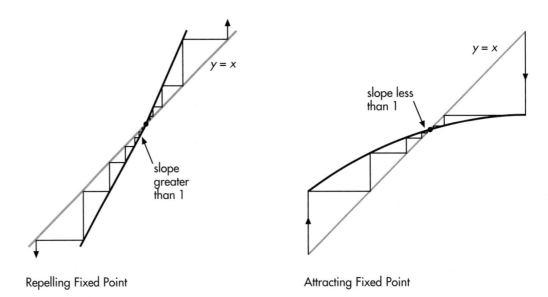

Repelling Fixed Point

Attracting Fixed Point

The slopes at fixed points can also be negative. If the slope is "not too negative," the fixed point will be attracting, but if the slope is very steep and negative, the fixed point will be repelling. Specifically, if the slope is between −1 and 0, the fixed point will be attracting, but if the slope is less than −1, the fixed point will be repelling.

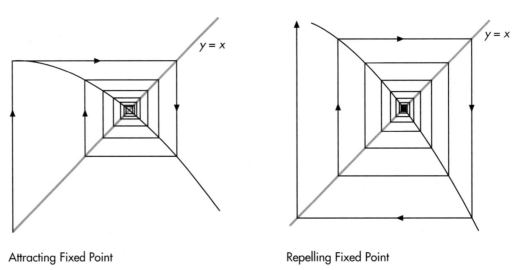

Attracting Fixed Point

Repelling Fixed Point

For example, the graph of $y = x^2 - 0.5$ shows that there are two fixed points. The fixed point on the right is clearly repelling, since the slope is greater than 1. To determine the type of the second fixed point, we could use graphical iteration as shown on the next page.

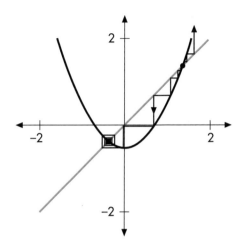

If we magnify the graph near this second fixed point, we see that the graph becomes straighter and straighter with the slope between 0 and −1. So the second fixed point is attracting.

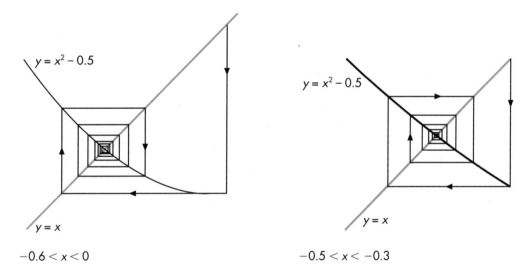

$-0.6 < x < 0$ $-0.5 < x < -0.3$

To summarize: A fixed point of an iteration rule is attracting if the slope of the graph at the fixed point is between −1 and +1. It is repelling if the slope is either greater than +1 or more negative than −1. Of course, the big question is: How do you compute the slope of the tangent line to the graph of a nonlinear expression? Luckily, this is exactly the question that calculus answers. When you study differential calculus, you will see that the derivative (one of the most important operations in calculus) gives precisely the slope we desire.

NEUTRAL FIXED POINTS

As in the case of linear iterations, there are some special cases when the graph has a fixed point at which the slope is either $+1$ or -1. In these cases, the fixed point may be attracting, repelling, or neither of these, in which case we have a neutral fixed point. For example, the graph of $y = x^2 + x$ has a fixed point at $x = 0$. From the right, this fixed point looks repelling, but from the left it appears to be attracting. Therefore, 0 is neither attracting nor repelling: It is a neutral fixed point.

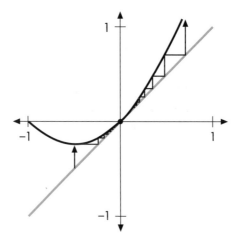

If you look at the graph of $y = x + x^3$, you see that this graph is tangent to the diagonal at the fixed point at 0, but graphical iteration shows that this fixed point is repelling:

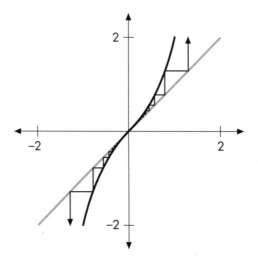

CYCLES

As we have seen, orbits may also cycle or tend to cycles with different periods. Cycles are very similar to fixed points in the sense that their orbits contain only a finite number of points. However, finding cycles algebraically is usually extremely difficult or impossible. For example, consider the iteration rule $x \rightarrow x^2 + c$. To find 2-cycles for this rule, we must first iterate twice

$$x \rightarrow x^2 + c \rightarrow (x^2 + c)^2 + c$$

and then solve the equation

$$(x^2 + c)^2 + c = x$$

This involves finding the roots of the fourth-degree equation

$$x^4 + 2cx^2 - x + c^2 + c = 0$$

which can be done (provided $c \leq -\frac{3}{4}$). See Investigation 5. To find **3-cycles,** however, we must iterate one more time:

$$x \rightarrow x^2 + c \rightarrow (x^2 + c)^2 + c \rightarrow ((x^2 + c)^2 + c)^2 + c$$

Now the resulting equation has degree 8:

$$((x^2 + c)^2 + c)^2 + c = x$$

This equation is impossible to solve algebraically, and we will not even bother to simplify it.

FINDING CYCLES GEOMETRICALLY

Often we do not need to know the exact location of cycles. Rather, we just need to know that they are present. This means that we can use graphical techniques to detect cycles. For this, it is best to use functional notation. Suppose $F(x) = x^2 + c$. Then we write $F^2(x) = F(F(x))$ as shorthand for the second iteration of the rule. So $F^2(x) = (x^2 + c)^2 + c$. Similarly, $F^3(x) = F(F(F(x)))$ is the third iteration, so $((x^2 + c)^2 + c)^2 + c$. In general, $F^n(x)$ is the nth iteration of the rule. That is, F^n denotes the n-fold composition of F with itself.

Now we merely have to graph $y = F^n(x)$ to find cycles of period n, for these cycles are given by solving $F^n(x) = x$. So, just as in the case of fixed points, we can see cycles of period n by looking for intersections of the graph $y = F^n(x)$

with the diagonal $y = x$. For example, if $F(x) = x^2 - 1$, the second iteration is given by

$$F^2(x) = (x^2 - 1)^2 - 1 = x^4 - 2x^2$$

To find where $y = F^2(x)$ intersects $y = x$, we solve $x^4 - 2x^2 = x$.

There are four real solutions at -1, 0, $(1 - \sqrt{5})/2$, and $(1 + \sqrt{5})/2$. Two of these solutions give fixed points of $F(x)$, namely, $(1 \pm \sqrt{5})/2$. The other points lie on a 2-cycle: 0 and -1. Using graphical iteration of F, we see these two fixed points as well as the 2-cycle:

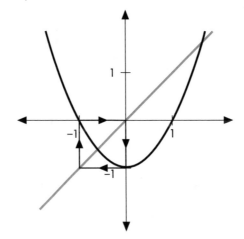

When we plot the graph of the second iteration and the diagonal $y = x$ we see these fixed points and cycles displayed as points of intersection of $y = F^2(x)$ and $y = x$:

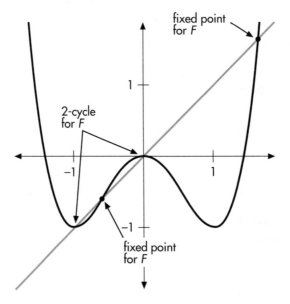

1 ▷ FATES OF ORBITS

Determine the fate of the orbit of 0 under the iteration rule $x \rightarrow x^2 + c$ for each of the following c-values.

$c = 0.3$: _____

$c = 0.2$: _____

$c = 0.0$: _____

$c = -0.5$: _____

$c = -1.1$: _____

$c = -1.3$: _____

$c = -1.38$: _____

$c = -1.6$: _____

$c = -1.76$: _____

$c = -1.77$: _____

$c = -1.8$: _____

2 ▷ GRAPHICAL ITERATION

Here is the graph of $y = x^2 - 1.3$. Using graphical iteration, sketch the orbit of 0 on this graph. (Use the results of Investigation 1.)

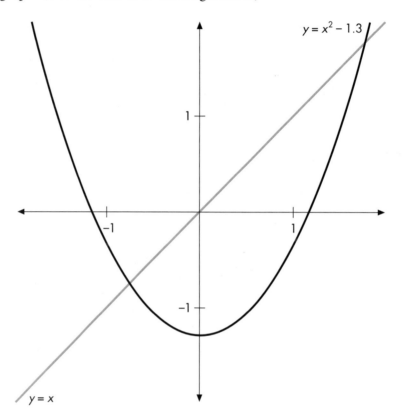

3 ▷ ESCAPING ORBITS

Here is the graph of $y = x^2 + c$ for a c-value with $c < -2$. Note how the graph pokes through the bottom of the box with vertices at (p_+, p_+) and $(-p_+, -p_+)$. We have shaded the interval of points along the diagonal that leave this box under one iteration of the rule $x \to x^2 + c$.

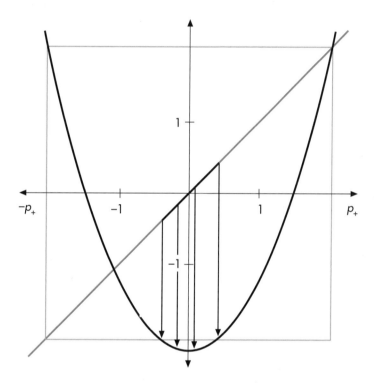

a. Using graphical iteration, find any interval along the diagonal whose orbit escapes from the box in exactly two iterations. Sketch these intervals on the graph on the following page. How many intervals do you find?

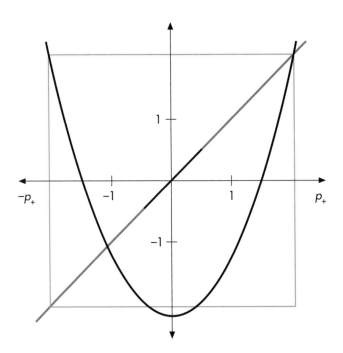

b. Now, using a different color, find the intervals that consist of points whose orbits leave the box in exactly three iterations. How many intervals do you find?

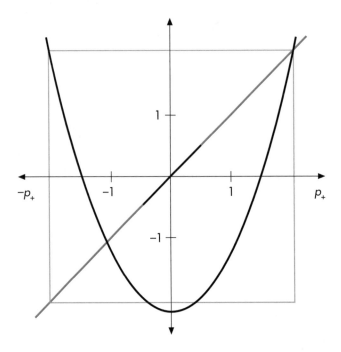

c. How many escape intervals do you expect to find after *n* iterations?

4 ▷ TYPES OF FIXED POINTS

Here are two graphs. In each case, use graphical iteration to determine whether each fixed point is attracting, repelling, or neutral.

a.

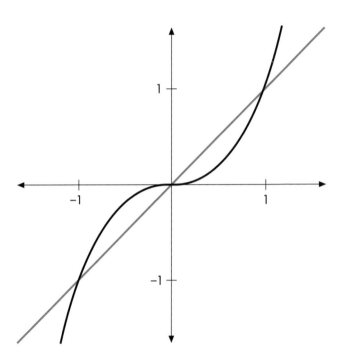

b.

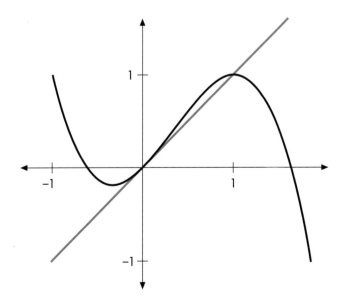

5 ▷ FINDING CYCLES GRAPHICALLY

Suppose $F(x) = x^2 - 2$. Use the graphs of $y = F^2(x)$ and $y = F^3(x)$ to determine how many fixed points, 2-cycles, and 3-cycles the iteration rule $x \rightarrow x^2 - 2$ has.

Graph of $y = F^2(x)$:

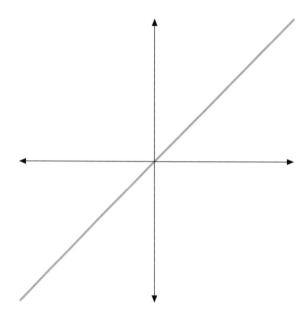

Graph of $y = F^3(x)$:

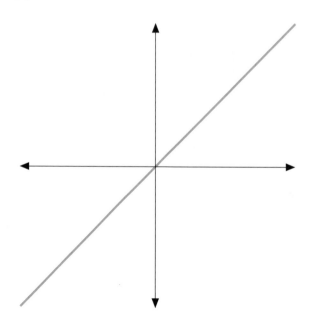

6 ▷ FINDING CYCLES ALGEBRAICALLY

Use algebra to determine for which values of c the iteration rule $x \rightarrow x^2 + c$
has a 2-cycle. _____

_____

_____

Complex Linear Iteration

OVERVIEW

This lesson is a review of complex numbers as well as complex linear iteration. Much of this material should be considered as review for the students, but it is important that it be covered to ease the transition from one-dimensional iterations to planar iterations.

MATHEMATICAL PREREQUISITES

Students need to be familiar with complex numbers and complex arithmetic. They should also be somewhat familiar with the geometry of the complex plane, including polar angle and magnitude. Students should certainly be comfortable with the fact that a complex number may be written in Cartesian form $x + iy$, and it is also useful, though not absolutely essential, that they understand the polar form $r\cos \theta + ir \sin \theta$.

MATHEMATICAL CONNECTIONS

This material connects well with an introduction to **complex numbers.** In particular, this lesson can be used as a stand-alone module involving **complex linear iteration.** For students who have used the book *Iteration* in this series, this material complements the lessons of that book dealing with linear iteration. In connection with a module on complex numbers, the lesson on complex linear iteration could end with a brief preview of nonlinear iteration and, in particular, with a few pictures of Mandelbrot and Julia sets. Using the polar form of complex numbers in this and the next lesson reinforces students' knowledge of trigonometry.

TECHNOLOGY

The Geometer's Sketchpad® can be used to view orbits of complex linear iteration. In addition, spreadsheets can be used to compute both the list of a complex orbit and a geometric display of the orbit as a sequence of points in the complex plane. Finally, recent calculators have the ability to work with and display complex numbers in familiar mathematical format.

SUGGESTED LESSON PLAN

CLASS TIME

This material can be covered in either one or two 50-minute sessions, depending on the students' familiarity with complex numbers. For students with a weak background in complex numbers, it would be appropriate to spend one session reviewing the arithmetic and geometry of complex numbers, paying specific attention to plotting complex numbers in the plane. A second period can be spent describing complex linear iteration, again with an emphasis on the plotting of orbits in the complex plane.

PREPARATION

The main goal of this lesson is to have the students understand the section "Geometry of linear iteration." It is essential that students be familiar with this section.

LESSON DEVELOPMENT

First review the arithmetic and geometry of complex numbers. Depending on the students' prior exposure to these concepts, the time this will take may vary. Investigations 1–3 are a review of complex numbers and can be assigned in class to check students' readiness to proceed.

Investigations 4 and 5 are important. Students have to become familiar with plotting orbits given by complex functions in order to fully comprehend the Mandelbrot and Julia sets. Investigations 6 and 7 also deal with this topic but involve trigonometry and the polar form of complex numbers.

Investigation 8 involves the fixed-point–based formula for linear iteration. It should be assigned only to students who fully understand this topic as described in the third book of this series, *Chaos*.

LESSON NOTES

For students who have no background in trigonometry, most material in this lesson is accessible, but certain sections should be skipped. Although it involves the polar form of complex numbers, Investigation 2 can be completed without recourse to trigonometry. Investigations 6 and 7 should not be assigned in this case. Also, much of the material in Lesson 3 will be inaccessible to students who do not have a trig background.

n previous books in this series, we have investigated many different types of iteration rules. Many times these iterations were defined by algebraic expressions into which we inserted numbers in order to compute orbits. In the previous books, these numbers were always real numbers. In this and the next few lessons, we will investigate what happens when the seed and/or the iteration rule involves complex numbers. We will see that allowing the iterations to be complex provides a far richer variety of fates for orbits.

REVIEW OF COMPLEX ARITHMETIC AND GEOMETRY

Let's pause to review a few ideas about complex numbers. Recall that a **complex number** is a number of the form $a + bi$, where a and b are real numbers and i is the imaginary number $\sqrt{-1}$. That is, i is the number whose square is -1, so $i^2 = -1$. For example, the numbers $3 + 2i$, $1 - 4i$, $2 + i$, and $3i$ are all complex numbers. We can even regard 7 as a complex number if we write $7 = 7 + 0i$. For a typical complex number $a + bi$, we have to specify the two numbers a and b. The number a is called the **real part** of the complex number; bi is called the **imaginary part** of the complex number.

Complex numbers are not "counting" numbers because unlike the real numbers, the complex numbers do not come with any particular linear order. Rather, complex numbers naturally "live" in the plane; we plot the complex number $a + bi$ in the Cartesian plane at the point whose coordinates are (a, b). Therefore, the numbers $2 + 3i$, $1 - i$, $2 - 3i$, $3i$, and -3 are plotted in the complex plane, as shown here:

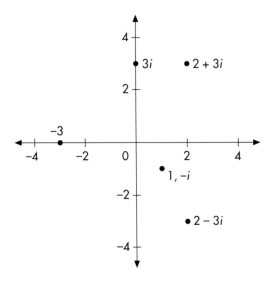

POLAR FORM

Since complex numbers reside in the plane, we may also describe these numbers in polar form. To do this, we must specify both the magnitude of the complex number and its polar angle. The **magnitude** of the complex number is simply the distance of the complex number from the origin. We denote the magnitude of a complex number by r. Using the distance formula, we see that the magnitude of $a + bi$ is $\sqrt{a^2 + b^2}$. For example, the magnitude of $2 + 3i$ is $r = \sqrt{2^2 + 3^2} = \sqrt{13}$.

The **polar angle** of a complex number is the angle formed by the positive x-axis and the straight line connecting the complex number to the origin. The angle is measured in the counterclockwise direction and is expressed in radians or degrees. We denote the polar angle by θ. For example, the polar angle of the complex number $2i$ is $\theta = 90°$. The polar angle of -2 is $\theta = 180°$. The polar angle of $1 + i$ is $\theta = 45°$, as shown here:

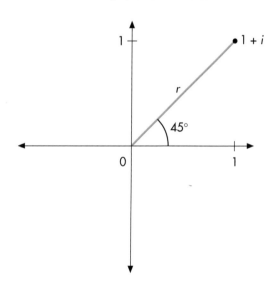

Note that if $a + bi$ is a complex number with polar angle θ and magnitude r, then a little trigonometry shows that

$$a = r \cos \theta$$

$$b = r \sin \theta$$

so that $a + bi = r \cos \theta + ir \sin \theta$. This expression is the **polar representation** of the complex number $a + bi$.

ARITHMETIC OF COMPLEX NUMBERS

We may add and multiply complex numbers as long as we follow the usual rules of algebra. For example, we add the two complex numbers $1 + 2i$ and $3 + 4i$ by adding their corresponding real and imaginary parts. So

$$(1 + 2i) + (3 + 4i) = (1 + 3) + (2 + 4)i = 4 + 6i$$

Complex multiplication is a little more involved. To multiply these two complex numbers, we use the usual rules of algebra, together with the fact that $i^2 = -1$ to find

$$(1 + 2i) \cdot (3 + 4i) = 1 \cdot 3 + 1 \cdot 4i + 2i \cdot 3 + 2i \cdot 4i$$

$$= 3 + 4i + 6i - 8$$

$$= (3 - 8) + (4 + 6)i = -5 + 10i$$

So the product of $1 + 2i$ and $3 + 4i$ is the new complex number $-5 + 10i$.

GEOMETRY OF COMPLEX MULTIPLICATION

It is important to be able to visualize the results of complex multiplication. For example, if we multiply the complex number $a + bi$ by 2, we find the new complex number $2a + 2bi$. Note that this number is twice as far from the origin as $a + bi$. If we multiply the number by –2, the result is $–2a – 2bi$, which is located twice as far from the origin, but on the opposite side of the origin. In general, we may use the polar representation of two numbers to determine the geometry of their product.

For example, if we have two complex numbers in polar form, say

$$a + bi = r_1 \cos \theta_1 + ir_1 \sin \theta_1$$

$$c + di = r_2 \cos \theta_2 + ir_2 \sin \theta_2$$

then their product is

$$(a + bi) \cdot (c + di) = r_1 r_2 \left(\cos \theta_1 \cos \theta_2 - \sin \theta_1 \sin \theta_2 \right)$$

$$+ ir_1 r_2 \left(\sin \theta_1 \cos \theta_2 + \sin \theta_2 \cos \theta_1 \right)$$

Using the trigonometric formulas for the sum of two angles, we see that

$$(a + bi) \cdot (c + di) = r_1 r_2 \big(\cos(\theta_1 + \theta_2) + i \sin(\theta_1 + \theta_2) \big)$$

This means that in order to multiply two complex numbers geometrically, we simply add their polar angles and multiply their magnitudes. For example, if we multiply the complex number $a + bi$ by i, we simply rotate $a + bi$ by 90° in the counterclockwise direction about the origin. The reason for this is that the magnitude of i is 1 and its polar angle is 90°. Similarly, if we square the complex number $a + bi$, we double its polar angle and square its magnitude. If we multiply a given complex number $a + ib$ by another complex number whose magnitude is greater than 1, the resulting product is a new complex number whose magnitude is larger than that of $a + ib$. Investigations 1–3 review these essential properties of arithmetic and complex numbers.

LINEAR COMPLEX ITERATION

Now let's use the arithmetic and geometry of complex numbers to investigate some simple complex iteration rules. Consider first the "simple" linear iteration $x \to 2x$. We know what happens if the seeds are real numbers: 0 is a repelling fixed point and all nonzero seeds lead to orbits that tend to positive or negative infinity. For example, the orbit of the seed 1 is

$$1 \to 2 \to 4 \to 8 \to 16 \to 32 \to 64 \to \cdots$$

If we choose a complex number for a seed, we can iterate in exactly the same way. For example, the orbit of the seed $1 + i$ is

$$1 + i \to 2 + 2i \to 4 + 4i \to 8 + 8i \to 16 + 16i \to \cdots$$

and the orbit of the seed $-2i$ is

$$-2i \to -4i \to -8i \to -16i \to -32i \to -64i \to \cdots$$

Note that each of these orbits moves farther and farther away from the origin as we iterate. For this reason, we also say that these orbits tend to infinity. Here we think of infinity as being "infinitely far from the origin" in the complex plane in any direction.

GEOMETRY OF LINEAR ITERATION

For real iteration rules, we have many geometric tools to help us "see" the fate of orbits. For complex iterations, this is no longer the case. For example, we cannot graph a complex iteration rule of the form

$$x \rightarrow Ax + B$$

if the numbers x, A, or B are complex numbers. Therefore, graphical iteration is not possible for these kinds of rules. Also, time series are much more difficult to visualize when the numbers involved are complex.

However, there is one tool that we can use to sketch the fate of these orbits. We can simply plot successive points on the orbit of a given seed in the plane and draw an arrow between them indicating the sequence of steps in the iteration. For example, for the iteration $x \rightarrow 2x$, we saw above that two orbits were

$$1 + i \rightarrow 2 + 2i \rightarrow 4 + 4i \rightarrow 8 + 8i \rightarrow 16 + 16i \rightarrow \cdots$$

and

$$-2i \rightarrow -4i \rightarrow -8i \rightarrow -16i \rightarrow -32i \rightarrow -64i \rightarrow \cdots$$

If we plot these orbits in the plane, drawing an arrow from each point to the next on the orbit, we see that each of these orbits escapes to infinity. In fact, note that each subsequent arrow is twice as long as the preceding arrow. This is because each iteration doubles the magnitude of the point on the orbit, while keeping the polar angle the same.

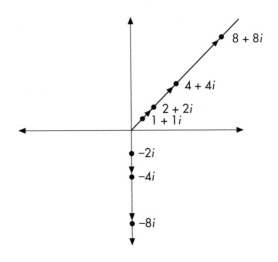

Using the geometry of complex multiplication, it is often easy to sketch the orbits of linear iterations. For example, for the iteration $x \to ix$, at each iteration we simply multiply the given complex number by i. This means that we increase the polar angle by 90°, while keeping the magnitude the same. As a consequence, all nonzero orbits rotate around the origin with period 4. For example, the orbit of $a + ib$ is

$$a + ib \to -b + ia \to -a - ib \to b - ia \to a + ib \to \cdots$$

which is a 4-cycle in the complex plane.

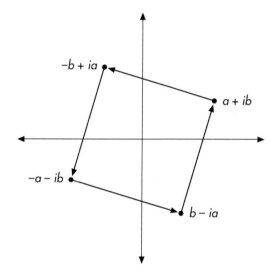

If we look at the iteration

$$x \to \left(\frac{1}{2} + \frac{1}{2}i\right)x$$

instead, then at each iteration we rotate points by 45° since the polar angle of $\frac{1}{2} + \frac{1}{2}i$ is 45°. At the same time, the points move toward the origin because the magnitude of $\frac{1}{2} + \frac{1}{2}i$ is $\frac{1}{\sqrt{2}}$, which is smaller than 1. For example, the orbit of 1 is

$$1 \to 0.5 + 0.5i \to 0.5i \to -0.25 + 0.25i \to -0.25 \to \cdots$$

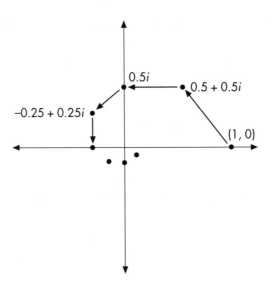

THE FATE OF COMPLEX ORBITS

For the moment, consider the simple complex linear iteration $x \rightarrow Ax$ where $A = a + bi$ is a complex number. Remember that the seed may also be a complex number, so each point on this orbit is actually a point in the plane. Note that this iteration has a fixed point at the origin, since $(a + bi) \cdot 0 = 0$. What is the fate of all other orbits? Well, that depends on the value of A.

We saw earlier that if the magnitude of $A = a + bi$ is greater than 1, then each time we multiply a number by $a + bi$, the resulting complex number has greater magnitude. That is, the orbit of any nonzero seed moves farther and farther from the origin. So these orbits tend to infinity. The origin is then a **repelling fixed point** for this iteration rule. For example, if $a + bi = 1 + i$, then all nonzero orbits of $x \rightarrow (1 + i)x$ tend to infinity since the magnitude of $1 + i$ is $\sqrt{2}$, as we see in the graph on the following page:

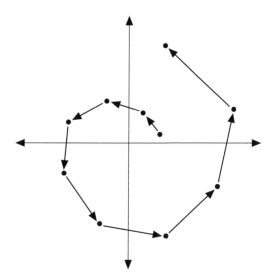

On the other hand, if the magnitude of $a + bi$ is less than 1, then each successive multiplication leads to a complex number with smaller magnitude, so iteration moves points on the orbit closer to the origin. In this case, 0 is an **attracting fixed point.** For example, if

$$a + bi = \frac{1}{2} + \frac{1}{2}i$$

then all orbits shrink toward 0 since the magnitude of $\frac{1}{2} + \frac{1}{2}$ is $\frac{1}{\sqrt{2}}$, which is less than 1. Thus, we see that the magnitude of $a + bi$ controls the fate of all orbits, at least when the magnitude of $a + bi$ is not equal to 1.

This observation is in exact agreement with what we saw for real linear iterations of the form $x \rightarrow Ax$. In this case, orbits tended to infinity if $|A| > 1$ and tended to 0 if $|A| < 1$. Of course, in the real case, $|A|$ is just the magnitude of A.

The only case that remains to consider is the case in which the magnitude of $a + bi$ is 1. In this case, multiplication by $a + bi$ does not change the magnitude of the seed. That is, each time we multiply, we merely rotate the given point by the polar angle of $a + bi$. For example, as we saw earlier for the iteration rule $x \rightarrow ix$, multiplication by i causes orbits to rotate by 90° in the counterclockwise direction. Similarly, multiplication by $\cos \theta + i \sin \theta$ makes orbits rotate around the origin by θ degrees at each iteration. As a consequence, all orbits remain on a circle around the origin. We call the origin in this case a **neutral fixed point;** orbits are neither repelled by nor attracted to this fixed point.

1 ▷ REVIEW OF POLAR REPRESENTATIONS

As a review, give the polar representation of each of the following complex numbers.

a. $-4i$ _____

b. $1 - i$ _____

c. $2 + 2i$ _____

d. 6 _____

e. $-2 - 2i$ _____

f. -15 _____

2 ▷ REVIEW OF COMPLEX GEOMETRY

The polar representation allows us to plot complex numbers just as easily as the Cartesian form. For each of the following magnitudes and polar angles, first compute the Cartesian form of the complex number, then plot each of these numbers in the plane, indicating both the polar angle and the magnitude.

$$a + bi$$

a. $r = 4, \theta = 180°$ _____

b. $r = 2, \theta = 45°$ _____

c. $r = 1, \theta = 135°$ _____

d. $r = 3.23, \theta = 270°$ _____

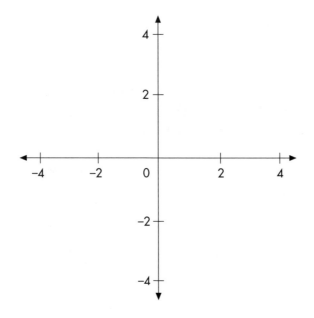

3 ▷ REVIEW OF COMPLEX ARITHMETIC

Just to make sure you have these concepts firmly in hand, compute these
complex numbers:

a. $(2 + 4i) + (3 - 2i) + 8i =$ _____

b. $4i \cdot (3 + 2i) =$ _____

c. $(2 + 4i) \cdot (3 - 2i) =$ _____

d. $(2 + 4i) \cdot (3 - 2i) \cdot 8i =$ _____

4 ▷ COMPLEX LINEAR ITERATION RULES

For each of the following linear iteration rules, compute the first eight points on
the orbit of the given seed. Then describe in a sentence or two the fate of the
orbit of that seed. Does it go to infinity? Does it go to a fixed point? Does it cycle?

a. $x \rightarrow x + i$, seed 0 _____

_____

_____

b. $x \rightarrow \frac{x}{2}$, seed $16 - 16i$ _____

_____

_____

c. $x \rightarrow -x - i$, seed 0 _____

_____

_____

d. $x \rightarrow ix$, seed $1 + i$ _____

_____

_____

e. $x \rightarrow ix + 1$, seed i _____

_____

_____

5 ▷ PLOTTING ORBITS IN THE COMPLEX PLANE

For each of the following iteration rules, plot the first eight points on the orbit of the given seed in the plane.

a. $x \rightarrow x + i$, seed $-1 - 4i$

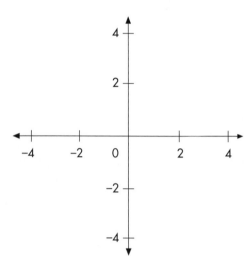

b. $x \rightarrow \frac{x}{2}$, seed $4 - 4i$

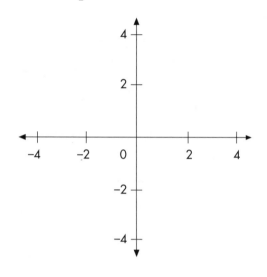

c. $x \rightarrow \frac{x}{2} + i$, seed $-4 - 4i$

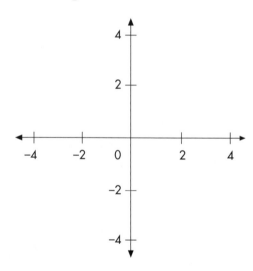

d. $x \rightarrow -x - i$, seed $1 + 2i$

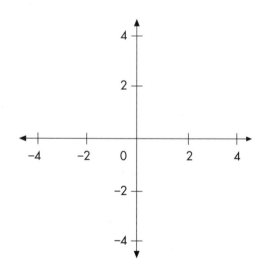

e. $x \rightarrow 2 + ix$, seed $1 + i$

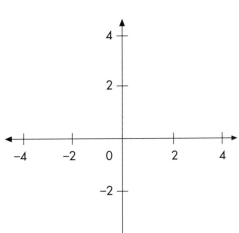

f. $x \rightarrow ix + 1$, seed i

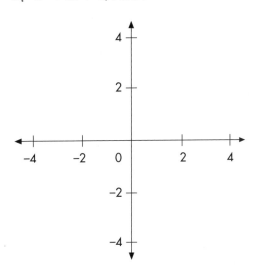

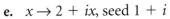

6 ▷ LINEAR ITERATION RULES

Describe the fate of all nonzero orbits in the complex plane under the following iteration rules. Use geometry to help you decide.

a. $x \rightarrow ix$

_____

_____

_____

b. $x \rightarrow (a + bi)x$ where the complex number $a + bi$ is given in polar form by $\cos \frac{\pi}{2} + i \sin \frac{\pi}{2}$

_____

_____

_____

c. $x \rightarrow (a + bi)x$ where the complex number $a + bi$ is given in polar form by $\cos \frac{2\pi}{3} + i \sin \frac{2\pi}{3}$

_____

_____

_____

d. $x \rightarrow (a + bi)x$ where the complex number $a + bi$ is given in polar form by $\cos \frac{2\pi}{5} + i \sin \frac{2\pi}{5}$

_____

_____

_____

e. $x \rightarrow (a + bi)x$ where the complex number $a + bi$ is given in polar form by $\cos \frac{2\pi}{79} + i \sin \frac{2\pi}{79}$

_____

_____

_____

f. Do you see some sort of pattern in parts a–e? What can you say in the general case where $a + bi$ is given in polar form by $\cos(2\pi\theta) + i \sin(2\pi\theta)$?

_____

_____

_____

7 ▹ ROTATIONS

In each case, determine the fate of all orbits under the iteration rule
$x \rightarrow (\cos(2\pi\theta) + i\sin(2\pi\theta))x$ for the given value of θ. Then sketch three
representative orbits using different colors for each.

a. $\theta = \frac{2}{5}$

_____

_____

_____

_____

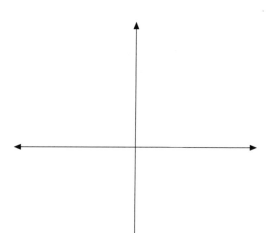

b. $\theta = \frac{3}{7}$

_____

_____

_____

_____

c. $\theta = \frac{1}{71}$

_____

_____

_____

_____

d. In a couple of sentences, describe the fate of orbits in case $\theta = \frac{p}{q}$ is a rational number.

_____

_____

_____

_____

8 ▷ GENERAL LINEAR ITERATION RULES

So far we have investigated linear iteration rules of the form $x \rightarrow Ax$ where A is a given complex number. The most general form of a linear iteration rule is $x \rightarrow Ax + B$ where now both A and B are complex numbers. Here we will explore what happens when these rules are iterated.

a. First find all fixed points for $x \rightarrow Ax + B$.

_____

_____

_____

b. Which values of A and B have no fixed points?

_____

_____

c. Which values of A and B have more than one fixed point?

_____

_____

d. Which values of A and B have only one fixed point?

_____

_____

The Squaring Rule

OVERVIEW

This lesson introduces the concept of a filled Julia set in the case of the very special iteration rule $x \rightarrow x^2$. This is essentially the only filled Julia set that can be computed by hand.

MATHEMATICAL PREREQUISITES

Students should be familiar with the results of iterating $x \rightarrow x^2$ when x is a real number. Essential use of polar angles and complex numbers in polar form $r \cos \theta + ir \sin \theta$ is made throughout the lesson. You can avoid this; however, that will obscure the mathematical connections with the usual squaring iteration rule.

MATHEMATICAL CONNECTIONS

This lesson relates to topics in **trigonometry** and the **geometry of complex numbers.** It can also serve as a useful stand-alone module for students learning complex arithmetic and geometry for the first time.

TECHNOLOGY

Spreadsheets or *The Geometer's Sketchpad* may be used to compute and display orbits under the squaring iteration rule, although it is certainly wisest to do this by hand at this stage. Also, numerous programs are available on the Web to compute Julia sets. See our Web site **http://math.bu.edu/DYSYS/toolkit** for an up-to-date list.

SUGGESTED LESSON PLAN

CLASS TIME

One 50-minute class period and a homework assignment should be sufficient to cover this material.

PREPARATION

The most important concept in this lesson is that of the filled Julia set. Students need to be able to articulate which points in the complex plane lie in the filled Julia set and which do not.

LESSON DEVELOPMENT

First review the fate of orbits for the real squaring iteration rule. This can be done without using graphical iteration if students are unfamiliar with this operation. Then review the geometry of complex multiplication and the special case of squaring.

Students should definitely work out Investigations 1 and 2. They should come away knowing which orbits do not escape (their seeds lie in the filled Julia set) and which orbits do escape (their seeds do not lie in the filled Julia set).

Transparency 3A can be used to display the results of Investigation 3.

The section "Revolutions" is optional, though accessible. It will not be used in subsequent lessons. However, if students have read about chaos in previous books in this series, then the squaring function on the circle provides another (especially simple) example of chaotic behavior. Similar behavior occurs on the Julia sets for any quadratic iteration rule, but it is not easy to show this. The cruel fact is that it is only the squaring iteration rule whose orbits are explicitly and easily computable by hand.

LESSON NOTES

Students need to be able to differentiate between three different ways to name points on the circle: radians, angles, and now revolutions. Investigations 5 and 6 are worthwhile exercises if students wish to pursue the squaring iteration rule on the Julia set further.

Three Seeds in the Complex Plane

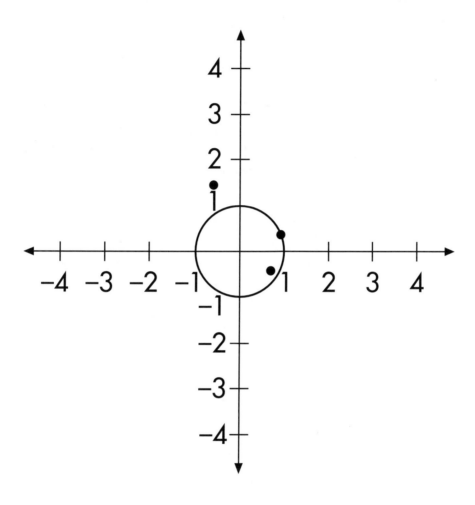

ow let's look at nonlinear iteration rules involving complex numbers. We will work with the complex version of the iteration rule $x \to x^2 + c$. We will see that this iteration rule leads to the fascinating geometric images known as the Mandelbrot set and Julia sets. Before tackling these difficult concepts, however, let's begin with a very special and simple case.

THE SQUARING ITERATION

Perhaps the simplest nonlinear iteration rule to understand is the squaring rule $x \to x^2$, that is, the case where $c = 0$. Recall that when the seeds for this rule are real numbers, then we understand the fate of all orbits. Using graphical iteration, we saw that given a seed x_0,

- the orbit tends to 0 (if $0 < |x_0| < 1$)
- the orbit goes to infinity (if $|x_0| > 1$)
- the orbit is fixed ($x_0 = 0$ or 1)
- the orbit is eventually fixed ($x_0 = -1$)

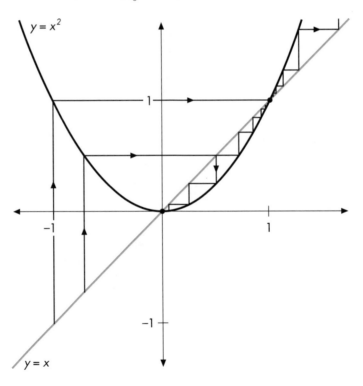

If the seed is a complex number, however, there are a number of additional possibilities. For example, if the seed is i, then the orbit is eventually fixed, but after two iterations

$$i \to -1 \to 1 \to 1 \to \cdots$$

The orbit of

$$\frac{-1 + \sqrt{3}\,i}{2}$$

lies on a 2-cycle because

$$\left(\frac{-1 + \sqrt{3}\,i}{2}\right)^2 = \frac{-1 - \sqrt{3}\,i}{2}$$

and

$$\left(\frac{-1 - \sqrt{3}\,i}{2}\right)^2 = \frac{-1 + \sqrt{3}\,i}{2}$$

The orbit of $-1 + \sqrt{3}\,i$ goes to infinity:

$$-1 + \sqrt{3}\,i \to -2(1 + \sqrt{3}\,i) \to 4(-1 + \sqrt{3}\,i) \to -8(1 + \sqrt{3}\,i) \to \cdots$$

Each successive point on this orbit jumps 180° as it gets farther and farther from the origin. Each point is a multiple of either $-1 + \sqrt{3}\,i$ or $1 + \sqrt{3}\,i$.

THE GEOMETRY OF SQUARING

If we write our seed in polar form as $x_0 = r(\cos \theta + i \sin \theta)$, then the orbit under squaring is relatively easy to compute. We know that when we multiply two complex numbers, we multiply their magnitudes and add their polar angles. Therefore, when we square a complex number, we simply square the magnitude and double the polar angle. So the orbit of x_0 in the complex plane is

$$x_0 = r(\cos \theta + i \sin \theta)$$

$$x_1 = r^2(\cos 2\theta + i \sin 2\theta)$$

$$x_2 = r^4(\cos 4\theta + i \sin 4\theta)$$

$$x_3 = r^8(\cos 8\theta + i \sin 8\theta)$$

and so on. At the nth step, we have

$$x_n = r^{2^n}(\cos 2^n\theta + i \sin 2^n\theta)$$

With this formula, we see that the complex squaring iteration does not differ very much from the real case for most seeds. If our seed has magnitude larger than 1, then $r > 1$ in the preceding expression. The orbit tends to infinity since r^{2^n} will get larger and larger. On the other hand, if the seed has magnitude less than 1 ($r < 1$), then the orbit tends to 0 because r^{2^n} becomes very small. So we understand the fate of all orbits under squaring, as long as the magnitude of the seed is not equal to 1.

If the magnitude is 1, then at this stage all we can say is that every point on the orbit also has magnitude 1. That is, if our seed lies on the circle of radius 1 centered at the origin, then the entire orbit lies on this circle. We will come back to this case in a moment. But first let's discuss the geometry of the orbits when $r \neq 1$.

Note that many orbits under squaring either spiral out to infinity or spiral inward toward 0, since at each iteration we double the polar angle. For example, the orbit of the seed $x_0 = 1.1\left(\cos(2\pi/5) + i \sin(2\pi/5)\right)$ is

$$x_0 = 1.1\left(\cos\left(\frac{2\pi}{5} \right) + i \sin\left(\frac{2\pi}{5} \right) \right)$$

$$x_1 = 1.21\left(\cos\left(\frac{4\pi}{5} \right) + i \sin\left(\frac{4\pi}{5} \right) \right)$$

$$x_2 = 1.4641\left(\cos\left(\frac{8\pi}{5} \right) + i \sin\left(\frac{8\pi}{5} \right) \right)$$

and so forth. At each stage the magnitude grows, and the successive polar angles are $2\pi/5$, $4\pi/5$, $8\pi/5$, and then $16\pi/5$, which represents the same angle as $16\pi/5 - 2\pi = 6\pi/5$. At the next iteration the polar angle is $12\pi/5$, which represents the same angle as $2\pi/5$. Thereafter, the polar angles begin to repeat after every fourth iteration. This does not mean that the orbit is a 4-cycle, however, since the magnitudes are growing at each stage. Rather, the orbit tends farther and farther from the origin at each iteration, so the orbit tends to infinity.

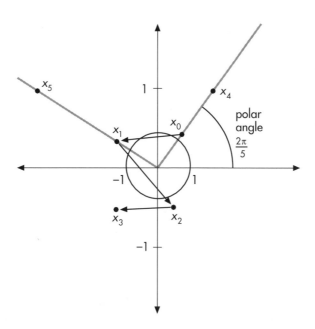

THE FILLED JULIA SET

From what we have done so far, we see that we can categorize orbits into one of two types: Either the orbit tends to infinity or it does not. We say that an orbit "escapes" if it tends to infinity. Those seeds that do not escape have a name: The collection of all of these seeds is called the **filled Julia set.** That is, the filled Julia set consists of those orbits that do not go to infinity. This set is named for the French mathematician Gaston Julia, who first studied these objects in the early twentieth century. In the case of the squaring iteration, the filled Julia set consists of all those seeds on and inside the circle of radius 1 centered at the origin. This is not a particularly interesting filled Julia set. In the next lesson, when we look at the quadratic iteration rule $x \rightarrow x^2 + c$ with c not equal to 0, we will encounter much more interesting filled Julia sets.

THE JULIA SET

For seeds in the filled Julia set, there are also two possibilities. One is that those seeds inside the circle of radius 1 tend to the attracting fixed point at the origin. The other possibility is that those seeds that lie exactly on the circle have orbits that stay on the circle forever. The circle of radius 1 is called the **Julia set** for this iteration rule. Another way to say this is that the boundary between the seeds whose orbits escape and those whose orbits do not is the Julia set.

It is unfortunate that the filled Julia set and the Julia set have names that are so similar. However, those names have become standard in the mathematical literature. One can use the more suggestive name "prisoner set" for the filled Julia set, since orbits in this set do not escape. Then the Julia set becomes the "boundary of the prisoner set." We choose not to adopt this terminology since there will be another prisoner set in a later section, namely, the Mandelbrot set. Two similarly named sets would lead to a lot of confusion.

ORBITS IN THE JULIA SET

So we understand the fate of all orbits under squaring with the exception of those on the Julia set, the circle of radius 1 centered at the origin. To investigate the fate of these orbits, we will resort to more geometry. Recall that if we have a complex number in polar form, the square of this number is given by doubling the polar angle and squaring the magnitude. Since our seed lies on the circle of radius 1 centered at the origin, squaring it does not change the magnitude. That is, when we iterate, the orbit of this point remains on the circle forever. Each time we iterate, we merely double the polar angle of the point on the circle. These orbits do not go to infinity nor do they go to the fixed point at the origin. So what happens to them?

REVOLUTIONS

The easiest way to figure out what happens to the orbits of seeds on the unit circle is to name the points on the circle by "revolutions" rather than by degrees or radians. We agree to start at the point 1 on the x-axis and call this angle 0 revolutions. The point located at -1 on the x-axis is halfway around the circle in the counterclockwise direction, so we say that it is located at $\frac{1}{2}$ of a revolution. The point i is located at $\frac{1}{4}$ of a revolution, and $-i$ is at $\frac{3}{4}$ of a revolution. If the number of revolutions becomes 1 or larger, we can reduce to an equivalent revolution between 0 and 1. For example, $\frac{7}{6}$ revolution is the same as $\frac{1}{6}$ revolution and 1 revolution is the same as 0 revolutions. The graph on the next page contains some points on the circle specified in revolutions.

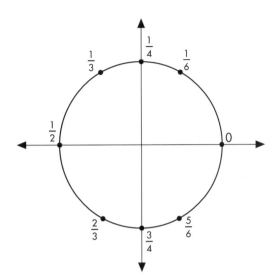

Be careful using these names. The point 1 on the x-axis is now called 0 revolutions. The point -1 on the x-axis is now called $1/2$ revolution. This can be confusing!

Now let's investigate orbits of the squaring iteration on the circle using revolutions. For example, if we start the seed $x_0 = i$, or rather, $1/4$ revolution, then the orbit is (in terms of revolutions)

$$\frac{1}{4} \to \frac{1}{2} \to 1 = 0 \to 0 \to 0 \to \cdots$$

so that this orbit eventually lands on the point located at 0 revolutions, which is a fixed point for $x \to x^2$. Note that at each iteration we simply double the number of revolutions, except that when we exceed 1 revolution we take only the fractional part of the number of revolutions. That is, 1 revolution is the same as 0 revolutions; $4/3$ is the same as $1/3$.

Now what happens when we begin at $1/3$ revolution? Doubling yields $2/3$ revolution, and doubling again yields $4/3$ revolutions, or $1/3$ revolution. That is, after two iterations we are back where we started, at $1/3$ revolution. So the orbit of $1/3$ under $x \to x^2$ is

$$\frac{1}{3} \to \frac{2}{3} \to \frac{1}{3} \to \frac{2}{3} \to \cdots$$

which is a cycle of period 2. We actually saw this orbit earlier for the point $-1/2 + \sqrt{3}i/2$ in the complex plane that corresponds to $1/3$ revolution around the circle.

If we begin with $\frac{1}{6}$, the orbit is

$$\frac{1}{6} \rightarrow \frac{1}{3} \rightarrow \frac{2}{3} \rightarrow \frac{1}{3} \rightarrow \frac{2}{3} \rightarrow \cdots$$

which starts at $\frac{1}{6}$ but then immediately begins to cycle with period 2. The orbit of $\frac{1}{12}$ eventually cycles with period 2 because the orbit is

$$\frac{1}{12} \rightarrow \frac{1}{6} \rightarrow \frac{1}{3} \rightarrow \frac{2}{3} \rightarrow \frac{1}{3} \rightarrow \frac{2}{3} \rightarrow \cdots$$

Similarly, the orbit of $\frac{3}{7}$ lies on a cycle of period 3:

$$\frac{3}{7} \rightarrow \frac{6}{7} \rightarrow \frac{5}{7} \rightarrow \frac{3}{7} \rightarrow \frac{6}{7} \rightarrow \frac{5}{7} \rightarrow \cdots$$

while the orbit of $\frac{3}{14}$ eventually cycles with period 3:

$$\frac{3}{14} \rightarrow \frac{3}{7} \rightarrow \frac{6}{7} \rightarrow \frac{5}{7} \rightarrow \frac{3}{7} \rightarrow \frac{6}{7} \rightarrow \frac{5}{7} \rightarrow \cdots$$

So we see that there are lots of cycles (and eventual cycles) in the Julia set of $x \rightarrow x^2$. But are there other kinds of orbits? So far, we have looked only at revolutions that are rational numbers, that is, numbers of the form p/q. What happens if we look at irrational numbers? Of course, this is difficult to do with a calculator or computer, since entering the infinitely many distinct digits in the decimal expansion of an irrational number takes a lot of time. We won't discuss it further here (you need advanced mathematics to do this), but the fact is that irrational numbers have orbits that never become cyclic. Some of these orbits wander around the circle, visiting every tiny arc of the circle, no matter how small. We saw such orbits in the third book in this series, *Chaos,* when we looked at histograms for chaotic orbits in the logistic iteration.

So we see that the fate of orbits on the Julia set of $x \rightarrow x^2$ is quite complicated. There are lots of cycles and eventual cycles intermingled with a great many chaotic orbits. On the other hand, off the Julia set, the fate of orbits is quite predictable. Outside the Julia set, orbits tend to infinity. Inside the Julia set, orbits tend to 0.

1 ▷ ORBITS UNDER COMPLEX SQUARING

Determine the fates of the following orbits under $x \to x^2$ by computing at least the first five points on the orbit of the given seed.

a. Seed: $x = -1$ _____

b. Seed: $x = 2i$ _____

c. Seed: $x = \frac{1}{2}i$ _____

d. Seed: $x = 1 + i$ _____

e. Seed: $x = \frac{1}{\sqrt{2}} + \frac{1}{\sqrt{2}}i$ _____

f. Seed: $x = \frac{1 + \sqrt{3}i}{2}$ _____

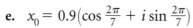

2 ▷ PLOTTING ORBITS

Plot six points on the orbits in the complex plane of each of the following seeds under $x \rightarrow x^2$. Use a different color for each.

a. $x_0 = 0.9\left(\cos \frac{2\pi}{3} + i \sin \frac{2\pi}{3}\right)$

b. $x_0 = 1.1\left(\cos \frac{2\pi}{3} + i \sin \frac{2\pi}{3}\right)$

c. $x_0 = \cos \frac{2\pi}{3} + i \sin \frac{2\pi}{3}$

d. $x_0 = 1.1\left(\cos \frac{2\pi}{7} + i \sin \frac{2\pi}{7}\right)$

e. $x_0 = 0.9\left(\cos \frac{2\pi}{7} + i \sin \frac{2\pi}{7}\right)$

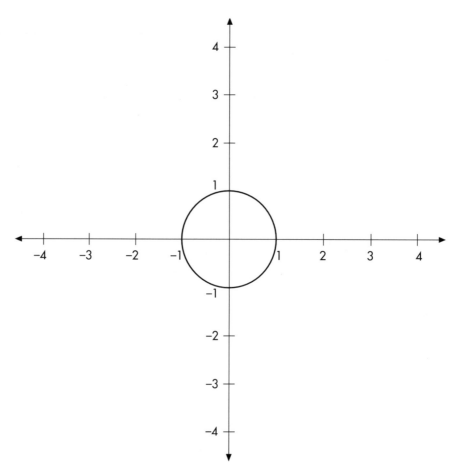

3 ▷ THREE SEEDS IN THE COMPLEX PLANE

In order to draw orbits under iteration of $x \rightarrow x^2$, you do not need to know the coordinates of the seed. Geometry is enough to draw these orbits. Here are three seeds in the complex plane. In each case, draw the next five points on the (approximate) orbits of these seeds under squaring.

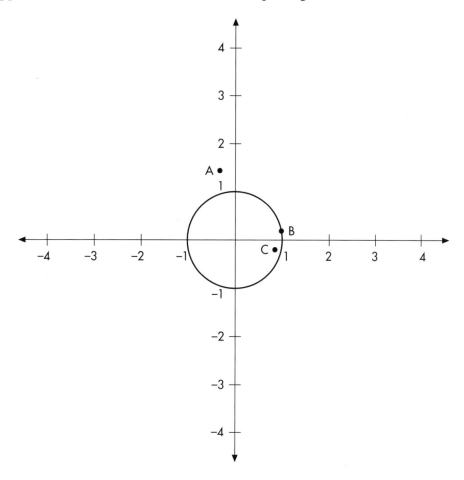

4 ▷ ORBITS ON THE UNIT CIRCLE

Each of these seeds represents a point on the unit circle described in revolutions. For each seed, decide if the orbit cycles (in which case, determine the period) or eventually cycles:

a. $\frac{1}{7}$ _____

b. $\frac{1}{9}$ _____

c. $\frac{1}{5}$ _____

d. $\frac{3}{28}$ _____

e. $\frac{1}{16}$ _____

f. $\frac{5}{11}$ _____

g. $\frac{7}{24}$ _____

5 ▷ ORBITS UNDER DOUBLING

a. Do you see a pattern in the previous Investigation? Pick a fraction p/q in lowest terms. What can you say about the orbit of p/q under doubling if q is odd?

_____

_____

b. What can you say if q is even?

_____

_____

6 ▷ FINDING CYCLES

Using revolutions, find all seeds on the unit circle whose orbits under doubling give cycles of the indicated period.

Period 1: _____

Period 2: _____

Period 3: _____

Period 4: _____

Period 5: _____

Period 6: _____

7 ▷ SENSITIVITY TO INITIAL CONDITIONS

What can you say about sensitivity to initial conditions for the iteration $x \rightarrow x^2$? Which seeds have orbits that behave sensitively in the sense that nearby orbits behave very differently?

_____

_____

_____

_____

Julia Sets of Quadratic Iterations

4

OVERVIEW

This lesson introduces the concept of a filled Julia set in the general case for the quadratic iteration rule $x \rightarrow x^2 + c$. We learn how these sets are computed and how the fate of the critical orbit affects the structure of these sets.

MATHEMATICAL PREREQUISITES

Students need to know the basics of iteration: orbits, fixed points, cycles. Familiarity with Lesson 2 is also a must. Although we do discuss the fractal nature of the Julia set, students need not know anything about fractals to understand this lesson. A solid grounding in algebra and the manipulation of inequalities is necessary to understand the final (optional) section called "The escape value."

MATHEMATICAL CONNECTIONS

Topics that have connections to material in this lesson include **inequalities, fractal geometry, computer algorithms,** and **iteration.**

TECHNOLOGY

This is where access to computers becomes essential. There are many software packages available to compute and draw filled Julia sets. Visit our Web site **http://math.bu.edu/DYSYS/toolkit** for an up-to-date list. The Mandelbrot Set Explorer at **http://math.bu.edu/DYSYS/explorer** contains a number of precomputed Julia sets and animations that are useful in studying this and the next two lessons. You might consider viewing the video *The Fractal Geometry of the Mandelbrot Set* while covering either this or the next two lessons.

Julia Sets of Quadratic Iterations

SUGGESTED LESSON PLAN

CLASS TIME

This mathematics is inherently more difficult than the mathematics in previous lessons. Moreover, technology is an essential ingredient of any lesson dealing with filled Julia sets. We allocate two class and/or computer lab sessions for this lesson.

PREPARATION

There are three major questions that need to be addressed in this lesson: (1) What exactly do the pictures of filled Julia sets represent? (2) How do we know when an orbit escapes to infinity? (3) What is the difference between a connected filled Julia set and fractal dust?

LESSON DEVELOPMENT

If you covered the previous lesson on the squaring rule in detail, students should have a good initial grasp of what a filled Julia set is. You can reinforce this understanding by immediately assigning the class activity to compute the filled Julia set of $x \rightarrow x^2 - 1$ by hand. Divide the students into groups and have them shade the squares depending on whether an orbit escapes or not. One way to do this is to place Transparency 4A on the overhead and have students compute various orbits and shade the corresponding seeds as they complete the task. Remember to stress that the seed is the center point of each box and that this point is of the form $\left(\frac{a}{10}, \frac{b}{10}\right)$ where $-16 \leq a \leq 16$ and $-8 \leq b \leq 8$.

The students should perform a specified number of iterations before deciding whether the orbit escapes. That number depends on what technology the students are using. If they are computing orbits by hand (ouch!), use no more than ten iterations. With a spreadsheet, many more iterations can be used. You will not get a very accurate picture of the filled Julia set by shading in this grid, but students should begin to understand via this method what the computer is actually doing when it displays filled Julia sets.

If completing this class activity is not feasible, you can substitute Investigation 1. Perhaps other seeds drawn from the transparency grid can be included in this assignment. The important thing for students to grasp is that there are two possibilities: either the orbit escapes or it does not.

Investigations 3–6 are very important. They will eventually lead to the definition of the Mandelbrot set. These are ideal lab assignments, given appropriate software. If you plan to cover the Mandelbrot set, be sure to assign Investigations 5 and 6, since they provide the basis for the definition of the Mandelbrot set.

LESSON NOTES

One temptation in drawing filled Julia sets using the computer is to use too many iterations. Students often use 1000 or more as a first choice for the number of iterations. This is unnecessary. Everyone becomes bored waiting for the computer to draw the results. Begin with 25 iterations and increase the number of iterations only gradually as you magnify the filled Julia sets.

The section called "The escape value" is optional. There we show mathematically why the escape criterion really works. In that section we use the triangle inequality in the form $|A + B| \geq |A| - |B|$.

This is equivalent to the usual form of the triangle inequality since

$$|A| = |A - B + B| \leq |A - B| + B$$

Subtracting $|B|$ from both sides yields this form of the inequality.

It is often quite difficult to determine visually whether or not a filled Julia set is connected. Two problems arise. First, sometimes it takes a large number of iterations to see the filled Julia set begin to disintegrate into fractal dust. If the c-value in question is close to the boundary of the Mandelbrot set (discussed in the next lesson), you will need many iterations (50 or more) for each seed to see the breakup. The rule of thumb is: If the picture begins to stabilize, then you can be fairly certain of the results. The section titled "Fractal dust" illustrates this.

The second problem is that certain filled Julia sets are "dendrites." These are essentially curves in the plane with infinitely many branches. Still, they are curves. As a consequence, it is difficult to see these sets using the escape-time algorithm mentioned in the Explanation. For example, the iteration rule $x \rightarrow x^2 + i$ has the property that the orbit of 0 does not escape (it eventually cycles with period 2), yet the filled Julia set is a dendrite.

There are other algorithms that do display this type of filled Julia set as a connected set (most notably the backward iteration algorithm), but this topic is one step beyond this text. In the Investigations, we have carefully selected c-values for which it is obvious whether the filled Julia set is connected or fractal dust.

Four transparency masters containing filled Julia sets are included. You can use these to investigate the self-similarity of filled Julia sets as well as to see the junction points.

Here is a perfectly acceptable rendition of the output of the class activity. You will most likely not receive results this accurate. That does not matter, however. The important thing is that students grasp the connection between what is in the filled Julia set and what is not.

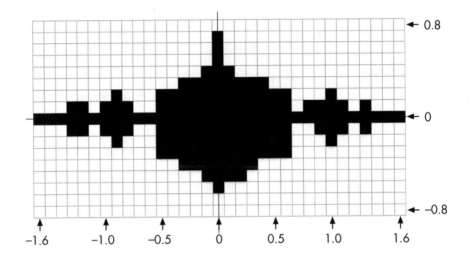

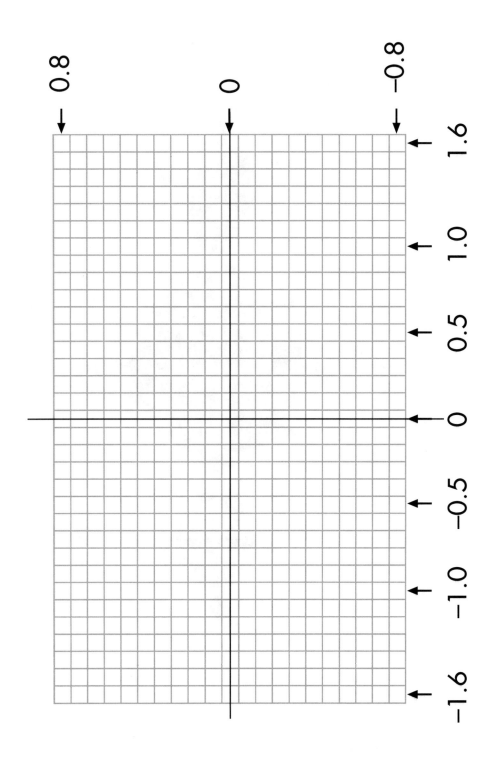

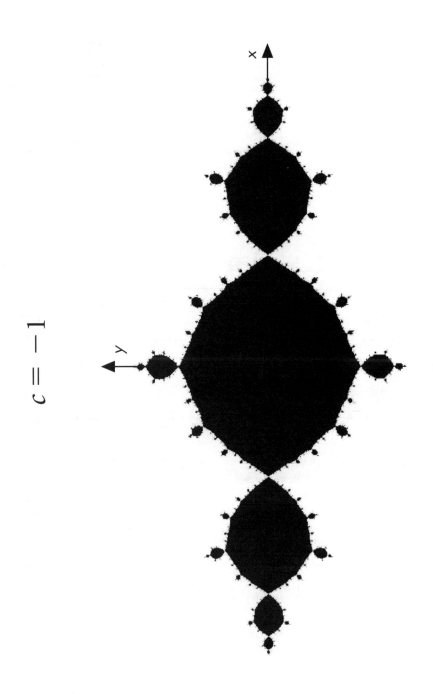

$c = -1$

$$c = -0.12 + 0.75i$$

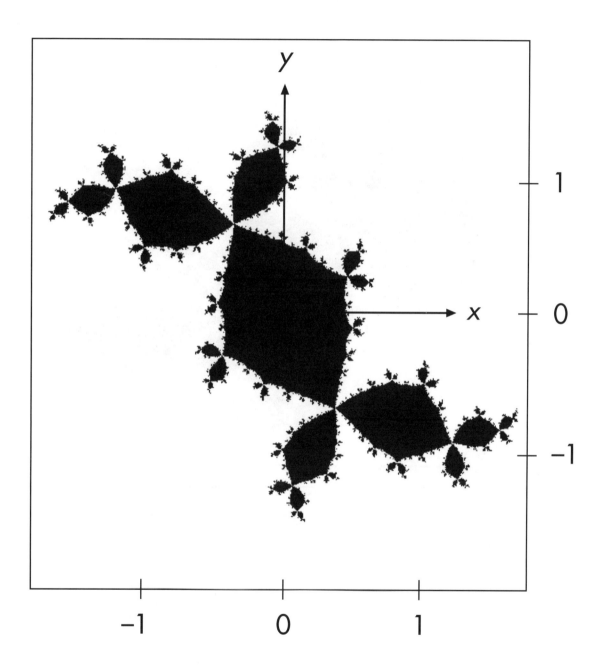

$$c = -0.5 + 0.57i$$

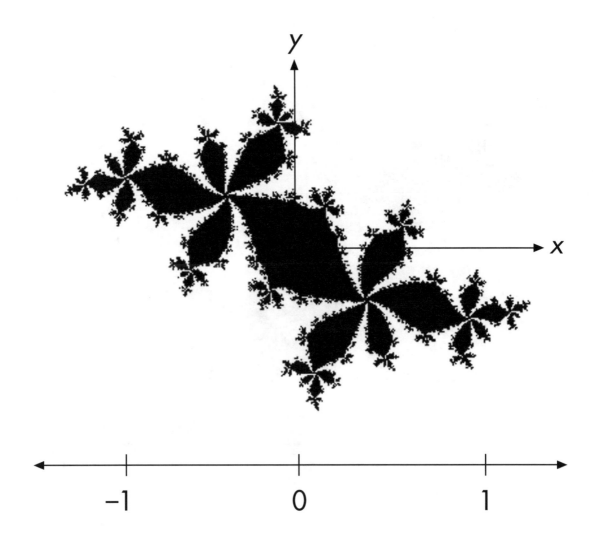

n the previous lesson, we investigated the fate of orbits of the simple iteration rule $x \to x^2$. We saw that we could separate orbits into two distinct classes: those that escaped to infinity (not in the filled Julia set) and those that did not escape (in the filled Julia set). Here we will attempt to do the same for the more general rule $x \to x^2 + c$. We will see that these iteration rules often produce very interesting and beautiful filled Julia sets.

In order to get the most out of this lesson, you really do need access to a computer and software that draws Julia sets. What computer and software you use does not matter, but the faster the computer, the better. Also, color monitors are very helpful in picking out the fine detail on a particular Julia set. If you have access to the Web, you can find some software for drawing Julia sets at **http://math.bu.edu/DYSYS/applets**. Be sure to look at the Mandelbrot Set Explorer at **http://math.bu.edu/DYSYS/explorer** as well.

A SPECIAL CASE

Let's begin with a special case, the iteration rule $x \to x^2 - 1$. The seeds -1 and 0 lie on a 2-cycle, since

$$0 \to -1 \to 0 \to -1 \to \cdots$$

The seeds i and $1 + i$ have orbits that tend to infinity, since

$$i \to -2 \to 3 \to 8 \to 63 \to \cdots$$

and

$$1 + i \to -1 + 2i \to -4 - 4i \to -1 + 32i \to -1024 - 64i \to \cdots$$

Finally, the seed $0.5i$ has an orbit that tends to the 2-cycle, since we have

$$x_0 = 0.5i$$

$$x_1 = -1.25$$

$$x_2 = 0.5625$$

$$x_3 = -0.6835\ldots$$

$$x_4 = -0.532\ldots$$

$$\vdots$$

$$x_{20} = -1.00000\ldots$$

$$x_{21} = 0.00000\ldots$$

As a consequence, the seeds 0, -1, and $0.5i$ all lie in the filled Julia set of $x \to x^2 - 1$, but the seeds i and $1 + i$ do not.

One question that comes up in this investigation is: How do we really know if an orbit does go to infinity? Yes, the complex numbers may be getting farther and farther from the origin, but how do we know that an orbit does not "double back" on us and stay close to 0?

THE ESCAPE VALUE

Actually, there is an easy answer to this question. If a point on the orbit of a seed x_0 ever has a magnitude that exceeds both 2 and the magnitude of the complex parameter c, then we automatically know that that orbit will go to infinity. The larger of the two numbers, 2 and the magnitude of c, is called the escape value for the iteration. We'll talk more about why this is true at the end of the lesson, but for now accept it as true and notice that this tells us when we can stop computing and decide that an orbit escapes.

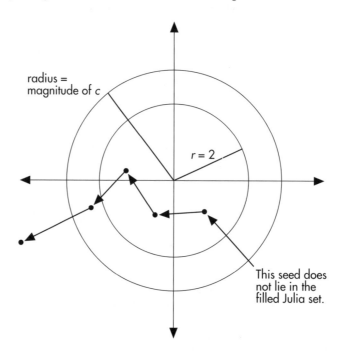

radius = magnitude of c

$r = 2$

This seed does not lie in the filled Julia set.

COMPUTING THE FILLED JULIA SET

This fact gives us an algorithm, or recipe, for computing the filled Julia set of $x \to x^2 + c$. We first determine which is the larger number, 2 or the magnitude of the given value of c. Next we divide the complex plane into a grid of complex numbers. Each point on the grid represents a seed. Then we turn on the computer and compute the orbits of each grid point. If a point on an orbit ever has a magnitude larger than the escape value, then we know that that orbit tends to infinity. As a consequence, the seed corresponding to this grid point does not lie in the filled Julia set. In practice, we usually choose a maximum number of iterations to perform on each seed. If the orbit exceeds the escape value before we reach this maximum number of iterations, we declare that the orbit has escaped and color the seed white. If the orbit does not reach the escape value during these iterations, we decide that the orbit does not escape and color the seed black. Of course, the orbit may escape after more iterations than our chosen maximum. For this reason, our picture of the filled Julia set may be inaccurate, as we will see below.

CLASS ACTIVITY

Before turning on the computer, let's get the hang of computing filled Julia sets by computing one by hand. Actually, it will be by lots of hands, since you will need the help of all of your classmates. Let's divide the plane into a grid of tiny squares. Each square will be exactly 0.1 unit in length and width, and the center of each box will be a point of the form $(a/10, b/10)$. Here is the grid that we will use:

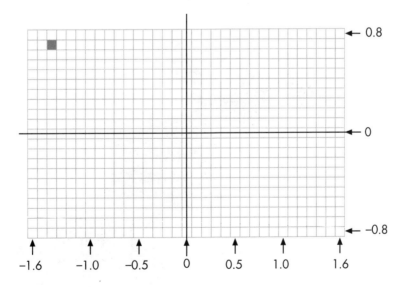

Note that the origin lies at the center of the central box in this grid. Also, the central point of the box that we have shaded is $(-1.4, 0.7)$. This corresponds to the complex number $-1.4 + 0.7i$. We will use this grid to paint the picture of the filled Julia set of the iteration rule $x \rightarrow x^2 - 1$. Divide this grid into enough different pieces so that each of your classmates has a number of points to work with. For example, each student might take one vertical column of grid points. The task is to compute the orbit of each seed corresponding to the central point in each square and to determine whether that seed escapes or not. If the seed escapes, then color the square in which the seed resides white (or red or blue, whatever is convenient). If the orbit does not escape, then color that square black. So black points will correspond to the filled Julia set of $x \rightarrow x^2 - 1$, while white points (or red, blue, etc.) will correspond to those seeds that escape.

THE FRACTAL RABBIT

This crude method of painting the picture of a Julia set does not do justice to the incredible structure of typical Julia sets. Below we display the Julia set of the quadratic iteration rule $x \rightarrow x^2 - 0.12 + 0.75i$. We have used a much finer grid for this picture, a grid of size 600 by 600 pixels in the portion of the plane satisfying $-2 \leq x \leq 2$ and $-2 \leq y \leq 2$. Thus, we used a total of 360,000 seeds, and we iterated each seed a total of 50 times to determine if the orbit escaped or not. We painted a seed black if the orbit of the seed did not escape and white if it did.

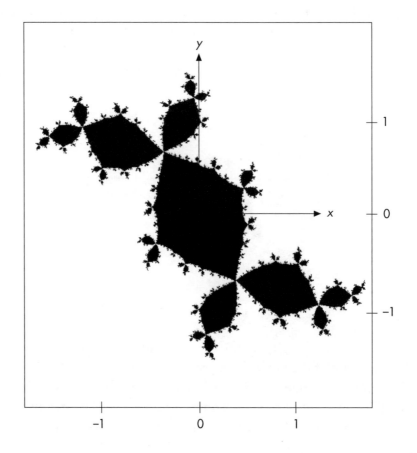

This filled Julia set is sometimes called "the rabbit" because it basically consists of a main body with two large "ears" attached. Well, not quite. There are two ears above and two ears below. But there is even more: Everywhere you look you seem to see smaller and smaller ears. So it is probably best to call this filled Julia set a "fractal rabbit." Here is a magnification of the upper left portion of this filled Julia set.

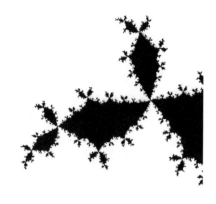

When we zoom in to the boundary of this filled Julia set, we see more and more pairs of ears. This is reminiscent of the fractal images we observed in the book *Fractals* in this series. Technically, it is the boundary of this set that is the fractal. Remember that we call the boundary of this set the "Julia set," so it is the Julia set of this quadratic iteration that possesses self-similarity. The filled Julia set (the entire black image) is not a fractal because we can zoom in to the middle and see all black. This is very different from the structure we see along the boundary, where we see ears attached to ears attached to ears, and so forth. Incidentally, this is an example of a connected filled Julia set because it consists of just one piece.

Here is another example. This is the filled Julia set corresponding to the iteration rule $x \to x^2 + 0.27 + 0.53i$. At first glance, this appears to be another fractal rabbit. But look more closely: This rabbit has three ears instead of two at each point. Again, this is a connected filled Julia set.

THE CRITICAL ORBIT

Recall that the orbit of 0 is called the **critical orbit** for the quadratic iteration. This is because 0 is the minimum for the graph of the real function $x \to x^2 + c$ (or, from calculus, where the derivative of the expression vanishes). As we will see, the orbit of 0 plays a very special role in determining the shape of the filled Julia sets. For the quadratic iteration $x \to x^2 - 0.12 + 0.75i$, we can compute the orbit of 0 and find

$$x_0 = 0$$

$$x_1 = -0.12 + 0.75i$$

$$x_2 = -0.668 + 0.57i$$

$$x_3 = -0.0015 - 0.011i$$

$$x_4 = -0.120 + 0.7499i$$

$$x_5 = -0.668 + 0.5698i$$

$$x_6 = 0.0016 - 0.0113i$$

$$x_7 = -0.120 + 0.7499i$$

Thus, the orbit of 0 tends very quickly to a 3-cycle given by

$$-0.120 + 0.7499i \to -0.668 + 0.5698i \to 0.0016 - 0.0113i \to -0.120 + 0.7499i \to \cdots$$

Pictorially, this 3-cycle looks like this:

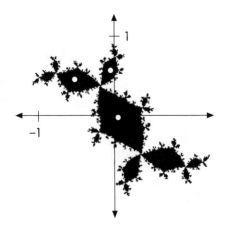

JUNCTION POINTS

Note that the fractal rabbit features infinitely many junction points where exactly three large black regions come together. If we remove any one of these points, the rabbit falls apart into three separate pieces. Notice that the period of the cycle to which 0 tends is also 3.

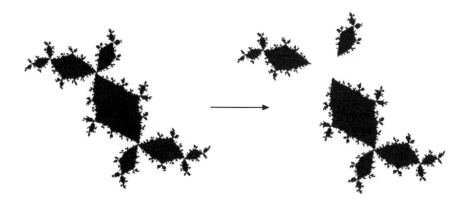

For the iteration rule $x \to x^2 + 0.27 + 0.53i$, a similar thing happens. This time the critical orbit tends to a 4-cycle after a number of iterations. The 4-cycle is given approximately by

$$0.0321 + 0.035i \to 0.269 + 0.532i \to 0.059 + 0.817i \to -0.394 + 0.627i \to 0.0321 + 0.035i \to \cdots$$

As above, we can break the filled Julia set into four pieces at each junction point:

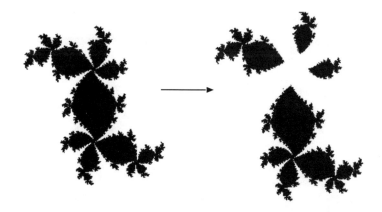

FRACTAL DUST

Certain filled Julia sets are difficult to see using our algorithm. They appear as a scatter of points in the plane or, sometimes, as nothing at all. Here is the filled Julia set associated with the iteration rule $x \rightarrow x^2 - 0.75 + 0.2i$. We computed this filled Julia set using 50 as the maximum number of iterations. Any black point in the plane has not "escaped" before iteration number 50. Notice that this filled Julia set does not appear to be connected.

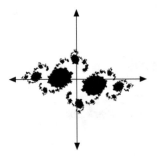

Watch what happens when we increase the number of iterations to 100: The filled Julia set appears to have separated into more pieces.

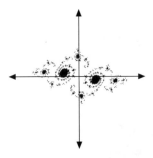

It also appears that the filled Julia set has shrunk. Now let's use 200 iterations:

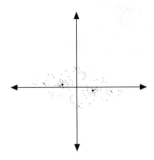

The filled Julia set is smaller still. It appears that if we increase the number of iterations, eventually all points will escape to infinity.

THE MANDELBROT AND JULIA SETS: A TOOL KIT OF DYNAMICS ACTIVITIES

Actually, this is not the case. There remains a set of points that do not escape. This set is called **fractal dust** because that's exactly what it is: a dust of points scattered around the complex plane. This is difficult to see on a computer screen because of the resolution of the screen. If we start with a seed close to, but not in, the filled Julia set, then this orbit will eventually escape. This eventual escape accounts for the shrinking we see on the preceding page.

EXPLOSIONS

The shape of the filled Julia sets for quadratic iteration rules can change dramatically as the parameter c is varied. For example, here is the filled Julia set for the iteration rule $x \rightarrow x^2 + 0.25$:

When we change the parameter to $c = 0.26$, the filled Julia set suddenly breaks apart into many different pieces, in fact, to fractal dust:

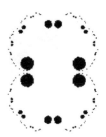

Here we have used a maximum number of 100 iterations to compute the filled Julia set. As on the preceding page, the large black regions in this picture shrink to dust as we increase the number of iterations.

Note that graphical iteration shows that the critical orbit escapes to infinity when $c = 0.26$, but it does not escape when $c = 0.25$. We will see the importance of this fact later.

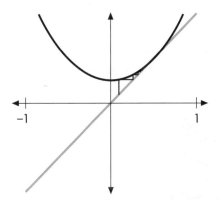

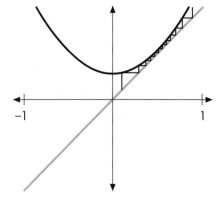

$c = 0.25$: critical orbit does not escape $c = 0.26$: critical orbit escapes

As another example, below we have computed the filled Julia set of the iteration rule $x \rightarrow x^2 - 0.75$.

But if we change the imaginary part of c ever so slightly to $c = -0.75 + 0.1i$, this picture emerges:

We used 150 iterations to compute this picture. Had we used more, the image would have disintegrated to fractal dust. In the case $x \rightarrow x^2 - 0.75$, you can check using graphical iteration that the critical orbit does not escape. However, when $c = -0.75 + 0.1i$, the critical orbit does escape to infinity. To see these explosions as animations, be sure to visit **http://math.bu.edu/DSYSY/explorer/**.

A LITTLE HISTORY

The extraordinary shapes of some of these Julia sets were first seen on the computer in 1980. However, that was not the first time mathematicians had studied Julia sets. During the period 1918–20, several French mathematicians began studying these objects. Among these mathematicians were Pierre Fatou and Gaston Julia, for whom the sets are named. These mathematicians were led to consider iterative rules in an attempt to solve certain "functional equations," a much more complicated type of equation than the usual algebraic equations you study in school today. Reading the old papers of these mathematicians shows that they could visualize the complicated shapes that Julia sets assume, despite the handicap of not having the computer or computer graphics to help them. However, it was difficult for these men to show the mathematical world the incredible beauty that they were seeing in their mind's eye and, as a consequence, interest in the Julia sets waned. All of that changed in 1980 when Benoit Mandelbrot, then a mathematician at IBM Thomas Watson labs, first used the power of the computer to explore these sets in detail.

THE ESCAPE VALUE

Previously we mentioned that we could be sure that an orbit escaped under the iteration rule $x \rightarrow x^2 + c$ if its magnitude ever exceeded the escape value. This value was the larger of 2 and the magnitude of the given value of c. To see why this is true, let's write $|x|$ for the magnitude of the complex number x. Warning! The following argument is not for the faint of heart!

Suppose that x_n denotes the nth point along an orbit and that we know $|x_n|$ exceeds the escape value. Expressing the triangle inequality as

$$|A + B| \geq |A| - |B|$$

which, by subtracting $|B|$ from both sides, is equivalent to

$$|A| = |A - B + B| \leq |A - B| + |B|$$

we have

$$|x_{n+1}| = |x_n^2 + c| \geq |x_n|^2 - |c|$$

Since $\left|x_n\right|$ is larger than the escape value, we know that $\left|x_n\right| > \left|c\right|$, or that by multiplying both sides by –1,

$$-\left|x_n\right| < -\left|c\right|$$

Therefore,

$$\left|x_{n+1}\right| \geq \left|x_n\right|^2 - \left|c\right| > \left|x_n\right|^2 - \left|x_n\right| = \left(\left|x_n\right| - 1\right)\left|x_n\right|$$

Now we also know that $\left|x_n\right| > 2$, so that $\left(\left|x_n\right| - 1\right) > 1$. Let's then say that $\left(\left|x_n\right| - 1\right) = D$ where D is some number that is larger than 1. Therefore, we know that

$$\left|x_{n+1}\right| > D\left|x_n\right|$$

That is, the magnitude of x_{n+1} exceeds that of x_n by a definite factor larger than 1.

Now let's do this again. Since the magnitude of x_{n+1} exceeds that of x_n, it follows that the magnitude of x_{n+1} also exceeds the escape value. So, by the preceding argument we know that

$$\left|x_{n+2}\right| > D\left|x_{n+1}\right|$$

But then

$$\left|x_{n+2}\right| > D^2\left|x_n\right|$$

Continuing in this fashion, we see that

$$\left|x_{n+k}\right| > D^k\left|x_n\right|$$

Now recall that $D > 1$, so the numbers D^k are growing. This means then that the magnitude of $\left|x_{n+k}\right|$ gets larger and larger, and so the orbit of our seed must escape to infinity.

THE MANDELBROT AND JULIA SETS: A TOOL KIT OF DYNAMICS ACTIVITIES

1 ▷ COMPUTING ORBITS

Compute the orbits of these seeds under $x \rightarrow x^2 - 1$ and determine their fates. You should use a computer or calculator to compute these orbits. Remember to use the escape value while making these computations! Determine whether these seeds are in the filled Julia set.

a. $x_0 = 1$

_____

_____

b. $x_0 = 0.2 - 0.2i$

_____

_____

c. $x_0 = -1 + 0.1i$

_____

_____

d. $x_0 = -1 + 0.4i$

_____

_____

2 ▷ COMPUTING FILLED JULIA SETS

Use a computer to compute the filled Julia set of the iteration rule $x \rightarrow x^2 - 1$. You should choose seeds $x + iy$ where $-2 < x, y < 2$ for this experiment. First compute this picture using a maximum number of iterations set at 25. Then use 50 iterations. Then use 100 iterations (assuming your computer is powerful enough to do this). Do you notice any significant difference between these images? Discuss in a paragraph any self-similarity you see.

_____

_____

_____

3 ▷ MATCHING FILLED JULIA SETS

Here are several c-values and several pictures of filled Julia sets. Match the c-values to the appropriate filled Julia set. You will need to have appropriate software to compute these filled Julia sets.

c-value	Filled Julia set
a. $-1 + 0.1i$	
b. $-0.5 + 0.55i$	
c. $0.38 + 0.34i$	
d. $-0.4 + 0.3i$	
e. $-0.64 + .423i$	
f. $0.24i$	
g. $0.4 + 0.22i$	
h. $0.125 + 0.62i$	

I.

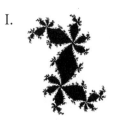

II.

III.

IV.

V.

VI.

VII.

VIII.

4 ▷ FATE OF THE CRITICAL ORBIT

For each of the c-values in Investigation 3, determine the fate of the critical orbit.

a. $c = -1 + 0.1i$

Fate: _____

b. $c = -0.5 + 0.55i$

Fate: _____

c. $c = 0.38 + 0.34i$

Fate: _____

d. $c = -0.4 + 0.3i$

Fate: _____

e. $c = -0.64 + 0.423i$

Fate: _____

f. $c = 0.24i$

Fate: _____

g. $c = 0.4 + 0.22i$

Fate: _____

h. $c = 0.125 + 0.62i$

Fate: _____

Discuss in a brief paragraph the relationship between the fate of the critical orbit and the geometry of the corresponding filled Julia set.

_____

_____

_____

5 ▷ FRACTAL DUST OR CONNECTED?

For each of these iteration rules, first compute the fate of the orbit of 0. Record whether the orbit escapes or not. Second, compute a picture of the filled Julia set for this rule. Third, discuss briefly the shape of the filled Julia set. Does it appear to be fractal dust? Or is it connected?

Rule	Fate
a. $x \rightarrow x^2 - 0.1 - 0.75i$	
b. $x \rightarrow x^2 + 0.12 - 0.75i$	
c. $x \rightarrow x^2 + 0.286 + 0.54i$	
d. $x \rightarrow x^2 + 0.486 + 0.54i$	
e. $x \rightarrow x^2 - 0.6 - 0.55i$	
f. $x \rightarrow x^2 - 0.5 - 0.55i$	
g. $x \rightarrow x^2 + 0.451 + 0.216i$	
h. $x \rightarrow x^2 + 0.392 + 0.216i$	
i. $x \rightarrow x^2 - 0.624 - 0.441i$	
j. $x \rightarrow x^2 - 0.23 + 0.45i$	

6 ▷ THE FUNDAMENTAL DICHOTOMY

Given the results of Investigation 5, what can you say about the relationship between the structure of the filled Julia set and the fate of the orbit of 0? This relationship is called the **fundamental dichotomy.**

_____

_____

_____

_____

7 ▷ THE c-PLANE

Think of the complex plane as the "c-plane." That is, each point in the plane corresponds to a different iteration rule of the form $x \to x^2 + c$. In this plane, plot the fate of the orbit of 0 for different c-values according to the following rule:

If the orbit of 0 escapes for a given value of c, then color c red. If 0 does not escape, then color c black.

Begin with the ten c-values that you used in Investigation 5. Then choose 15 additional c-values. For the moment, use only c-values that have a magnitude less than 2. Remember, you plot the c-values in the plane—not the orbit of 0.

The Mandelbrot Set

OVERVIEW

In this lesson we begin the study of the Mandelbrot set. Most of this section is devoted to Investigations.

MATHEMATICAL PREREQUISITES

Students need to be familiar with the filled Julia set. In particular they need to be familiar with the fundamental dichotomy (Investigations 5 and 6 in Lesson 4).

MATHEMATICAL CONNECTIONS

This lesson really belongs to the realm of experimental mathematics. Students will learn how to explore using the computer as a tool. They will also use reflective **symmetry.**

TECHNOLOGY

This lesson is best taught in a computer lab with all students having access to a computer with appropriate software. Check our Web site **http://math.bu.edu/DYSYS** for an up-to-date list of available software that will compute and display the Mandelbrot and Julia sets.

SUGGESTED LESSON PLAN

CLASS TIME

This lesson is best taught in one or two computer lab sessions. Have students work in groups on the various Investigations. Students can take turns inputting data into the computer and recording the results. The video *The Fractal Geometry of the Mandelbrot Set* can be substituted for computer lab experiments

if appropriate facilities are not available. However, if students do have computers available to perform these experiments, it is probably best not to show the video until after they have made the discoveries themselves.

PREPARATION

The most important concept in this lesson is the definition of the Mandelbrot set. Stress that the Mandelbrot set is a picture in the c-plane. It is the "parameter plane." The filled Julia set is quite different: It is the "dynamical plane." There is only one Mandelbrot set whereas there are infinitely many distinct filled Julia sets.

LESSON DEVELOPMENT

Begin by reminding students of the fundamental dichotomy. Then turn to the definition of the Mandelbrot set. It is helpful to perform Investigation 1 as a class so that students grasp the meaning of the Mandelbrot set. You can use Transparency 5A to indicate the c-value locations.

Then turn to the periods of the bulbs. Students should complete the diagram of periods in Investigation 4. They should then turn to Investigation 6 to discover that they can read off the periods of the bulbs simply by counting the spokes in the antenna. Finally, Investigation 7 duplicates the results found in Investigations 3 and 4 in Lesson 4. Nevertheless, this Investigation is important, especially if you plan to cover the next lesson.

LESSON NOTES

Students often ask why we use the orbit of 0 to paint the picture of the Mandelbrot set. The main reason is the fundamental dichotomy: It is the fate of the orbit of 0 that determines whether the filled Julia set is connected or fractal dust. There is also another reason to use the orbit of 0: If the iteration rule $x \rightarrow x^2 + c$ has an attracting cycle, then the critical orbit must be attracted to it. So this means that this rule can have at most one attracting cycle! Moreover, it is the orbit of 0 that finds the attracting cycle. Proofs of these facts are, unfortunately, well beyond the scope of this book. The proofs demand knowledge of complex calculus.

Nevertheless, students, especially those with programming experience, often wish to paint the Mandelbrot set using a different seed. They can do this and obtain a somewhat different picture than the Mandelbrot set. They should realize, however, that the picture they obtain tells them only about the fate

of the orbit of the particular seed that was chosen. Their picture has nothing to do with the structure of the filled Julia sets, which is the real reason the Mandelbrot set is so important.

STUDENT PROJECTS

The material in this and the next lesson provides a wealth of opportunities for class activities. Here are some possible activities:

1. Make the world's largest picture of a Mandelbrot set. Have various groups of students compute and print various regions of the Mandelbrot set and then assemble these images to form a huge Mandelbrot set. Of course, students computing regions inside the main cardioid will not have too much fun, so it might be best to choose carefully the regions to be explored.

2. On a large picture of the Mandelbrot set, compute and display the periods of as many bulbs as are visible.

3. On a large picture of the Mandelbrot set, display small pictures of associated filled Julia sets with arrows pointing to the bulb from which they came (the bulb containing the appropriate c-value).

The Mandelbrot set

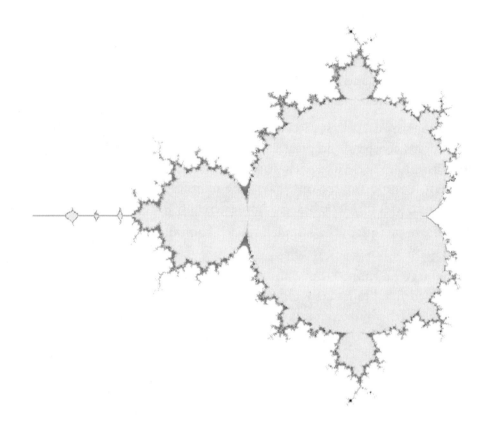

ow we turn to the study of one of the most beautiful and complicated objects in all of mathematics, the Mandelbrot set. Ever since its image was first generated and viewed in 1980, this set has been the subject of intensive research. Mathematicians have now come to understand much of the intricate geometry of this set, but even today some portions of this object defy comprehension. In fact, if you look deeply enough into the Mandelbrot set, you may be the first person ever to view certain portions of this set. What is more important, however, is that you begin to understand the mathematics behind this object.

THE FUNDAMENTAL DICHOTOMY

Recall from Lesson 4 that for the complex iteration rule $x \to x^2 + c$, the orbit of 0—the critical orbit—plays a fundamental role. If the orbit of 0 escapes to infinity, then the corresponding filled Julia set for that c-value is hardly visible on the computer. It consists of a scatter of points that we call fractal dust (or technically, a Cantor set). On the other hand, when the orbit of 0 does not go to infinity, the filled Julia set is one connected piece and its boundary, the Julia set, is often a fractal. So the fate of the orbit of 0 tells us a great deal: It tells us the basic shape of the corresponding filled Julia set. For example, here is the filled Julia set for the iteration rule $x \to x^2 - 0.49 + 0.58i$:

In this case, the orbit of 0 tends to the 5-cycle given by

$$-0.501 + 0.570i \rightarrow -0.574 - 0.001i \rightarrow -0.17 + 0.571i \rightarrow$$

$$-0.798 + 0.376i \rightarrow -0.005 - 0.029i \rightarrow -0.501 + 0.570i \rightarrow \cdots$$

Note that this filled Julia set is a connected set.

On the other hand, when we change the parameter value to $-0.5 + 0.65i$, the filled Julia set suddenly explodes and becomes fractal dust. In this case, the orbit of 0 tends to infinity.

THE MANDELBROT SET

As a consequence, it makes sense to ask what the set of all complex c-values for which the orbit of 0 does not escape looks like. This set, called the **Mandelbrot set,** is a picture of certain c-values in the complex plane. It can be thought of in two different ways. On the one hand, it is a picture of those c-values for which the corresponding filled Julia set is connected. It is also a picture of those c-values for which the corresponding orbit of 0 under $x \rightarrow x^2 + c$ does not go to infinity.

For example, the c-value 0 is in the Mandelbrot set because for the iteration rule $x \rightarrow x^2 + 0$, 0 is a fixed point. So the orbit of the critical point, 0, certainly does not escape. Also, as we saw earlier, the filled Julia set for $x \rightarrow x^2 + 0$ consists of all points on and inside the circle of radius 1 centered at the origin in the plane. Similarly, the c-value -1 is in the Mandelbrot set because the orbit of the critical point, 0, lies on a 2-cycle $0 \rightarrow -1 \rightarrow 0 \rightarrow \cdots$.

Below is a picture of the Mandelbrot set. Notice that the entire picture lies inside the circle of radius 2 centered at the origin. The tail lies at the point $-2 + 0i$. The real-number axis is a line of symmetry, but the imaginary axis is a little off-center.

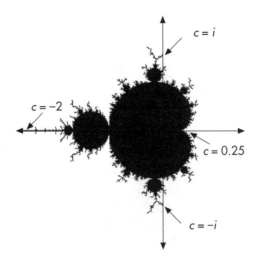

THE PRINCIPAL BULBS

The main piece of the Mandelbrot set looks like an apple on its side. This region is called the **main cardioid** of the Mandelbrot set because its boundary is similar to the curve known in mathematics as a cardioid.

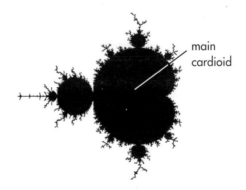

Attached to the main cardioid are numerous **bulbs** or **decorations.** Each decoration features a large circular region from which many more decorations extend. Also, there is a large antenna-like structure attached to each bulb. In the middle of each antenna, there is a point called the **junction point** from which several different "spokes" emanate.

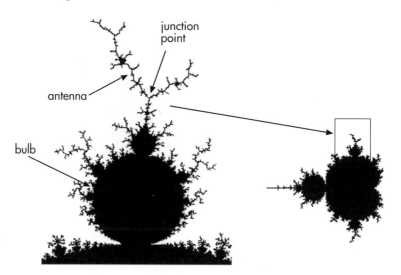

At the top of the main cardioid is what we call the **period-3 bulb.** The period-3 bulb gets its name from the fact that if we choose any c-value within the largest circular region in this bulb, then the orbit of the critical point, 0, for this c-value tends to a cycle of period 3. For example, in Lesson 4 we worked with the iteration rule $x \rightarrow x^2 - 0.12 + 0.75i$. We saw that the c-value $-0.12 + 0.75i$ led to a filled Julia set that we called the fractal rabbit and the orbit of 0 tended to a 3-cycle. This c-value is located near the middle of the period-3 bulb. If you choose c-values that do not lie in the large black circular region here, you find different fates. However, all c-values within this largest circular region have the property that the orbit of 0 tends to a 3-cycle.

TECHNOLOGY TIP

There are some online explorations available at the Web site for the Mandelbrot Set Explorer—**http://math.bu.edu/DYSYS/explorer.** Be sure to check them out! Some of the applets at the Web site **http://math.bu.edu/DYSYS/applets** can also be used to help with some of these investigations.

1 ▷ LOCATING *c*-VALUES

Using the table on the following page, determine which of the following *c*-values lie in the Mandelbrot set by computing the fate of the corresponding critical orbit. Recall that this means you need to compute the orbit of 0 under the iteration rule $x \rightarrow x^2 + c$ and then determine whether or not the orbit tends to infinity. Then locate these *c*-values in or around the picture of the Mandelbrot set below.

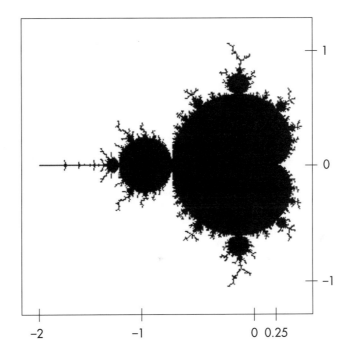

	c-value	In the set?	Fate of the orbit of 0
a.	$-0.12 - 0.75i$		
b.	$0.12 - 0.75i$		
c.	$0.286 + 0.54i$		
d.	$0.486 + 0.54i$		
e.	$-0.515 + 0.56i$		
f.	$-0.7 + 0.56i$		
g.	$0.385 + 0.333i$		
h.	$0.585 + 0.333i$		
i.	$-0.624 + 0.441i$		
j.	$-0.23 + 0.45i$		
k.	i		
l.	$2i$		
m.	-1.3		
n.	$1 + i$		
o.	0.26		
p.	-2		

2 ▷ THE MAIN CARDIOID

a. Choose several c-values from within the main cardioid of the Mandelbrot set. Then use a computer to compute the orbit of 0 for each of these c-values as well as the corresponding filled Julia set. Record your findings.

c-value	Fate of the orbit

b. Describe the similarities of each filled Julia set for your c-values.

_____

_____

_____

_____

c. Based on these observations, what do you conclude about the behavior of the critical orbit for any c-value inside the main cardioid?

_____

_____

_____

_____

3 ▷ THE PERIOD-3 BULB

Each of the following c-values belongs to the period-3 bulb discussed in this lesson. First compute the fate of the orbit of 0 for the following c-values, and then locate each c-value in the period-3 bulb.

c-value	Fate of the orbit
$-0.014 + 0.812i$	
$-0.186 + 0.743i$	
$-0.060 + 0.704i$	

4 ▷ PERIOD-*k* BULBS

Each of the bulbs attached directly to the main cardioid has a characteristic cyclic property as in Investigation 3. If you choose any *c*-value from within the largest black region in a bulb, the fate of the orbit of 0 is always the same. The critical orbit always tends to a cycle with some given period, say, period *k*. We then call this bulb a **period-*k* bulb.** For each of the indicated bulbs in the Mandelbrot set below, determine the period of the bulb. Choose more bulbs if you have time.

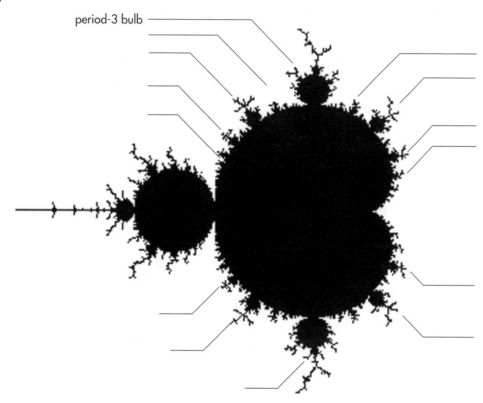

period-3 bulb

5 ▷ SYMMETRY IN THE MANDELBROT SET

What symmetry, if any, do you notice in the Mandelbrot set and in the fates of the orbit of the critical orbit?

_____

_____

_____

6 ▷ GEOMETRY OF THE BULBS

Look closely at each bulb. Each of them is different in appearance. Make a conjecture about how to "read off" the period of the bulb simply by looking at the geometry of the bulb.

_____

_____

_____

_____

What are the periods of the following bulbs?

a. Period = _____   **b.** Period = _____

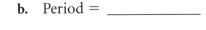

c. Period = _____   **d.** Period = _____

e. Period = _____   f. Period = _____

7 ▷ FILLED JULIA SETS AND PERIODS OF BULBS

We saw in Investigation 3 that any filled Julia set from the large black region in the period-3 bulb at the top of the Mandelbrot set looked like our friend, the fractal rabbit. Is there a way, by simply looking at the filled Julia set, to determine the period of the bulb from which it came?

_____

_____

_____

_____

Find the periods of the bulbs from which each of the following filled Julia sets came.

a. _____   b. _____

c. _____

d. _____

e. _____

f. _____

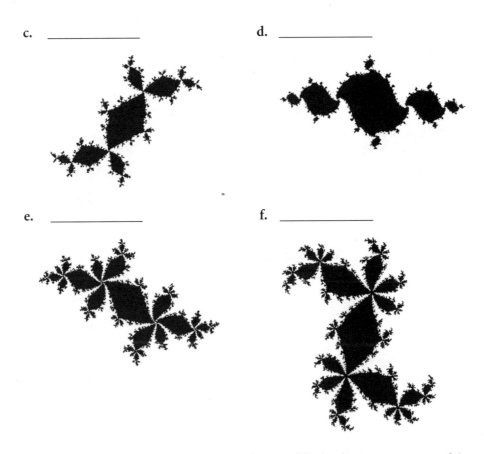

Indicate the bulbs from which each of these filled Julia sets came on this Mandelbrot set:

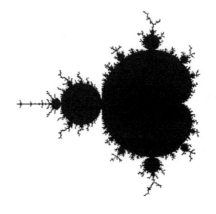

Geometry of the Mandelbrot Set 6

OVERVIEW

In this lesson, we continue the study of the Mandelbrot set. Here we show several more facts about the fascinating geometry of this set.

MATHEMATICAL PREREQUISITES

Students need to be familiar with Lessons 4 and 5.

MATHEMATICAL CONNECTIONS

This lesson really belongs to the realm of experimental mathematics. Students will continue to explore using the computer as a tool. Along the way they will see the **Fibonacci sequence** and find both **rational and irrational numbers** on the graph of the Mandelbrot set.

TECHNOLOGY

This section is best taught in one or two computer lab sessions with all students having access to a computer with appropriate software. Check our Web site **http://math.bu.edu/DYSYS** for an up-to-date list of available software that will compute and display the Mandelbrot and Julia sets.

SUGGESTED LESSON PLAN

CLASS TIME

Have students work in groups on the various Investigations. They can take turns inputting data into the computer and recording the results for the nine Investigations. The video *The Fractal Geometry of the Mandelbrot Set* can be substituted for computer lab experiments if appropriate facilities are not available. However, if students do have computers available to perform these experiments, it is probably best not to show the video until after they have made the discoveries themselves.

Instead of simply telling the students how to count and how to add bulbs, have them discover these facts themselves. Investigations 4–6 allow students to see that the bulbs are arranged around the cardioid in the exact order of the rationals. Investigation 7 deals with the addition of rotation numbers. The main point of the video *The Fractal Geometry of the Mandelbrot Set* is to show dynamically these two facts.

PREPARATION

The Explanation section is fairly long and detailed. Before you present the material in this section, it is best to have performed some of the experiments ahead of time.

LESSON DEVELOPMENT

The main topic in this lesson is rotation numbers. Students should be able to read off the rotation number in three ways:

1. from the geometry of the cycle to which 0 is attracted,
2. from the arrangement of the "ears" on the filled Julia set, and
3. from the arrangement of the "antennas" on the bulb in the Mandelbrot set.

Investigations 1–3 facilitate finding rotation numbers. Students do not need to have elaborate computer programs available to complete these Investigations.

LESSON NOTES

As mentioned in the Explanation, determining the rotation number of a bulb from its antenna structure sometimes fails. This happens most often for bulbs near the cusp of the main cardioid (between 0 and $\frac{1}{5}$ and between $\frac{4}{5}$ and 1). There is a way to measure these lengths and then determine the corresponding fraction, but this involves using a different (non-Euclidean) length—a topic beyond the scope of this book.

A curious way of adding fractions appears in mathematics in many different forms. This is what is known as the Farey tree or Farey sequence, after John Farey (1766–1826), an English civil engineer and mathematician. In number theory, you can determine the fraction between two given fractions that has the smallest denominator in the following manner. Start with 0 and 1,

which we write as fractions $^0/_1$ and $^1/_1$. Any two adjacent fractions in the list below are called "Farey neighbors." Given two Farey neighbors, they immediately become "Farey parents" and produce a "Farey child." The Farey child is derived in one of two ways: either by Farey addition (adding the numerators and adding the denominators) or by choosing the fraction between the parents that has the smallest denominator. Amazingly, these two numbers are the same.

For example, at the outset, $^0/_1$ and $^1/_1$ are neighbors. They become parents of $^1/_2$. Note that $^1/_2$ is indeed the fraction between the parents with the smallest denominator. Now we have this list of fractions:

$$\frac{0}{1} \qquad\qquad \frac{1}{2} \qquad\qquad \frac{1}{1}$$

Continuing, $^0/_1$ and $^1/_2$ produce $^1/_3$ while $^1/_2$ and $^1/_1$ give $^2/_3$.

So the next stage of the Farey tree is

$$\frac{0}{1} \qquad \frac{1}{3} \qquad \frac{1}{2} \qquad \frac{2}{3} \qquad \frac{1}{1}$$

and so on:

$$\frac{0}{1} \quad \frac{1}{4} \quad \frac{1}{3} \quad \frac{2}{5} \quad \frac{1}{2} \quad \frac{3}{5} \quad \frac{2}{3} \quad \frac{3}{4} \quad \frac{1}{1}$$

What a delight! Of course, one has to wonder about the pedagogical implications of teaching students to add this way! Be sure to caution students that this special way of adding fractions works only in this setting.

STUDENT PROJECTS

As in the previous lesson, the material in this lesson provides a wealth of opportunities for class activities. Here are two interesting activities:

1. Compute a variety of $^p/_q$ bulbs and filled Julia sets and arrange them in order with the corresponding fraction below. You have painted a picture of the number line in a rather different way!

2. On a large picture of the Mandelbrot set, compute and display the rotation numbers of as many bulbs as are visible.

As we are beginning to see, there is a beautiful and unexpected relationship between the geometry of the Mandelbrot set and the filled Julia sets. But there is even more to this story. In this lesson, we'll investigate this relationship in more detail.

TECHNOLOGY TIP

You might wish to watch the video titled *The Fractal Geometry of the Mandelbrot Set* while reading this explanation, or perform some of the explorations at the Mandelbrot Set Explorer Web site: **http://math.bu.edu/DYSYS/explorer**.

ROTATION NUMBERS

Let's look in more detail at the cycle to which the orbit of 0 (the critical point) tends when we choose a c-value from within one of the bulbs attached to the main cardioid. For example, consider the period-3 bulb at the top of the Mandelbrot set and choose a c-value from within that bulb, say, $c = -0.12 + 0.75i$ as we considered earlier. (Remember that we always choose the c-value from within the largest circular region, not any of its satellite decorations.) Then we compute the 3-cycle toward which the orbit of 0 tends and watch how this cycle jumps around the filled Julia set. The 3-cycle is given by

$$0.0016 - 0.0113i \rightarrow -0.120 + 0.7499i \rightarrow -0.120 + 0.7499i \rightarrow 0.0016 - 0.0113i \rightarrow \cdots$$

x_0	$0.0016 - 0.0113i$
x_1	$-0.120 + 0.7499i$
x_2	$-0.120 + 0.7499i$
x_3	$0.0016 - 0.0113i$

If we display this orbit in the corresponding filled Julia set, we find this
fractal rabbit:

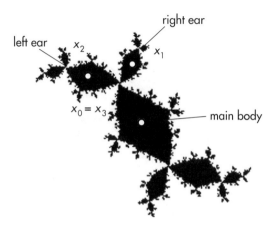

The orbit of this cycle moves from the "main body" of the rabbit, into the
right upper ear of the rabbit, then into the left upper ear of the rabbit, and
then it repeats the pattern. Roughly speaking, this cycle winds around the
junction point joining the ears and the main body by making $\frac{1}{3}$ of a turn in
the counterclockwise direction at each iteration. For this reason, we say that
this orbit has rotation number $\frac{1}{3}$. In fact, every filled Julia set that arises from
a c-value in the largest circular region in the top bulb on the Mandelbrot set
has rotation number $\frac{1}{3}$. For that reason, we rename this bulb the $\frac{1}{3}$-**bulb.**

We may in similar fashion assign a rotation number to each bulb attached to
the main cardioid. This rotation number is a fraction of the form p/q where q
is the period of the bulb in question and p tells us how the orbit of the cycle
rotates around the filled Julia set in the counterclockwise direction. That is, the
"ears" containing the q-cycle are rotated by p/q turns around the junction point
at each iteration.

To understand this naming procedure, consider another example: Choose
c-values from two different period-5 bulbs in the Mandelbrot set. The first
c-value is $c_1 = -0.5 + 0.56i$ and the second is $c_2 = 0.39 + 0.34i$. In each case,
the orbit of 0 tends to a 5-cycle that we call

$$x_0 \rightarrow x_1 \rightarrow x_2 \rightarrow x_3 \rightarrow x_4 \rightarrow x_0 \rightarrow \cdots$$

Note that the locations of c_1 and c_2 in the Mandelbrot set lie in different bulbs:

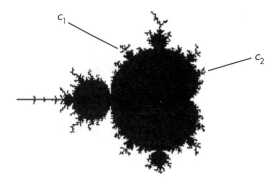

The filled Julia sets corresponding to each of these c-values are quite different in appearance. Also, the rotation numbers differ. Here is the filled Julia set and cycle corresponding to $c = c_1$.

This filled Julia set is hardly a rabbit, but we can still make out the main body (containing the point x_0). Now the main body has four ears attached. At each iteration, the cycle makes a $2/5$ jump in the counterclockwise direction. In other words, at each iteration the cycle jumps over one ear to get to its destination. For this reason, c_1 lies in the $2/5$-bulb.

Below is the filled Julia set and cycle corresponding to $c = c_2$.

This time the behavior of the cycle is different. At each iteration, we rotate by approximately $\frac{1}{5}$ of a turn in the counterclockwise direction. We do not jump over any ears as we rotate. For this reason, c_2 comes from the $\frac{1}{5}$-bulb.

USING YOUR EYEBALLS TO FIND ROTATION NUMBERS

You can actually determine the rotation number directly from the geometry of the filled Julia sets, at least for cycles with low period. Note that in each of the preceding examples, the cycle begins in the main body of the set and then moves to the smallest "ear" after one iteration. So we can measure the rotation number at this jump simply by finding the smallest ear and judging its position relative to the main body.

For example, the filled Julia set corresponding to $c = -1$ is

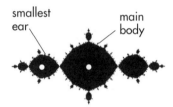

This filled Julia set comes from the $\frac{1}{2}$-bulb since the smallest ear is located $\frac{1}{2}$ turn from the main body.

In a more illustrative example, consider the filled Julia set corresponding to $c = 0.29 - 0.54i$. There is a 4-cycle that attracts the orbit of 0 in this filled Julia set. Note that the smallest ear containing the 4-cycle lies in the ear that is located $\frac{1}{4}$ of a turn from the main body in the clockwise direction, or $\frac{3}{4}$ of a turn in the counterclockwise direction. For this reason, this c-value lies in the $\frac{3}{4}$-bulb.

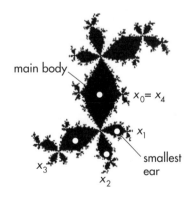

In the preceding example, not only does the smallest ear in the filled Julia set contain x_1, but the next largest ear contains x_2 and so forth. This means that we do not even have to see the cycle in order to identify the rotation number. For instance, the filled Julia set pictured below comes from the $^4/_7$-bulb since the smallest ear is located $^4/_7$ of a turn in the counterclockwise direction from the main body. (You don't know whether the cycle lies in the "upper" or "lower" ears, but it doesn't matter: The smallest is located $^4/_7$ of a turn in either case.) Note again how the ears increase in size as you continue to rotate by $^4/_7$ of a turn:

So we see that we can identify the rotation number associated with each bulb in two ways: from the structure of a filled Julia set corresponding to a c-value inside the bulb attached to the main cardioid, and from the behavior of the cycle toward which the orbit of 0 tends when c is chosen within that bulb.

A word of caution is necessary here: This method of determining rotation numbers does not always work. Certain bulbs (particularly those near the "cusp" of the main cardioid) have certain elongated ears that cause erroneous computations of the rotation number. The foolproof method is to use the geometry of the cycle.

ANOTHER WAY TO FIND ROTATION NUMBERS

There is one other way to identify the period of the bulb. This method, like the one described previously, is not really rigorous in that it does not always work, but it can give a way of recognizing certain bulbs quickly. Look at both the $1/3$- and $2/5$-bulbs in the Mandelbrot set:

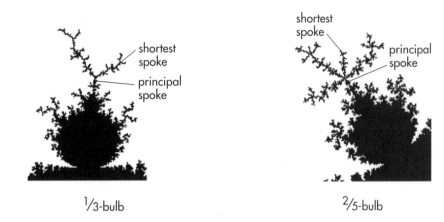

$1/3$-bulb $2/5$-bulb

Look at the antennas of each of these bulbs. From the junction point, a number of spokes emanate. If you count them, you see exactly the number corresponding to the period of the bulb. Note that one spoke emanates from the bulb itself and connects the junction point to the bulb. This spoke is called the **principal spoke.** Now notice the location of the shortest spoke (not including the principal spoke). In the $1/3$-bulb, this spoke is located approximately $1/3$ of a turn in the counterclockwise direction from the principal spoke. In the $2/5$-bulb, you must make a $2/5$ turn to reach the shortest spoke. As another example, here is the $3/7$-bulb. Again we see that the shortest spoke is located $3/7$ of a turn in the counterclockwise direction from the principal spoke:

Now this method does not always work well, as shown by the $1/4$-bulb:

It is not clear which is the shortest spoke in this picture, though it is clear that the longest is located $3/4$ of a turn in the counterclockwise direction. Sometimes this method simply fails. For example, here is the $11/12$-bulb:

Twelve spokes emanate from the junction point, but it does not appear that the spoke located $11/12$ of the way around is the shortest. So you have to be careful when you use this method. It is really useful only when used with the two other methods of finding rotation numbers.

HOW TO COUNT

So far we have found the rotation numbers corresponding to seven different c-values. These come from different bulbs attached to the main cardioid. In the picture on the following page, we have indicated the location of these bulbs. Note that beginning on the positive horizontal axis and moving counterclockwise around the boundary of the main cardioid, these bulbs are arranged in the order of the real numbers. That is, the order of the bulbs is $1/5$, $1/4$, $1/3$, $2/5$, $3/7$, $3/4$, $11/12$, and $1/5 < 1/4 < 1/3 < 2/5 < 3/7 < 3/4 < 11/12$.

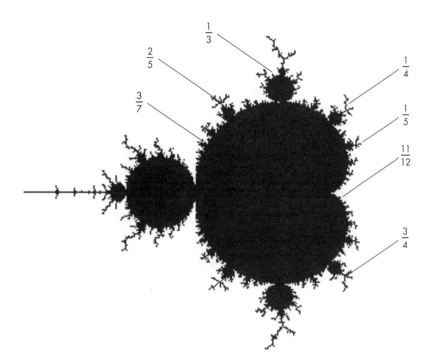

Is this order of bulbs a coincidence? We urge you to perform Investigations 5 and 6 to explore this further.

HOW TO ADD

The following "coincidence" will knock your socks off. Let's look at the relative sizes of the bulbs and, in particular, the "largest" bulb between two given bulbs. For example, the largest bulb between the $\frac{1}{2}$- and $\frac{1}{3}$-bulbs is the $\frac{2}{5}$-bulb:

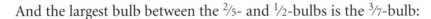

And the largest bulb between the ²/₅- and ¹/₂-bulbs is the ³/₇-bulb:

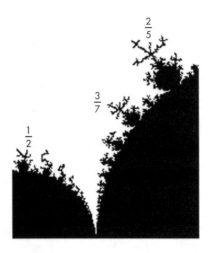

Notice that you can obtain the largest bulb between the ¹/₂-bulb and the ¹/₃-bulb by adding the fractions the "wrong" way—that is, by adding the numerators and adding the denominators. The numerators add up to 2 and the denominators to 5, and the ²/₅-bulb is the largest in between. The same thing happens in the second example: Add the numerators and denominators of ¹/₂ and ²/₅ to obtain ³/₇, which just happens to be the largest bulb between the ¹/₂- and ²/₅-bulbs. Could this be true? Go to Investigation 7 to find out.

At this point, we have only begun to scratch the surface of the mathematics behind the Mandelbrot set. We have worked only with the principal bulbs. But there are many other bulbs and small copies of the Mandelbrot set buried within the entire set. Using geometric and counting techniques just like we have used above, we can begin to understand how the Mandelbrot set is assembled. See, for example, Investigations 8 and 9. At this point, you might wish to strike off on your own and investigate other areas of the Mandelbrot set. Who knows what treasures you might find!

THE FIBONACCI SEQUENCE

There is so much in the Mandelbrot set. We can even find the famous Fibonacci sequence 1, 1, 2, 3, 5, 8, 13, . . . in the Mandelbrot set. Forget about the fractions for a moment and think only of the periods of the bulbs (the denominators). In Investigation 7, we saw that we can add these denominators to find the period of the largest bulb between two given bulbs. This is precisely the prescription that leads to the Fibonacci sequence:

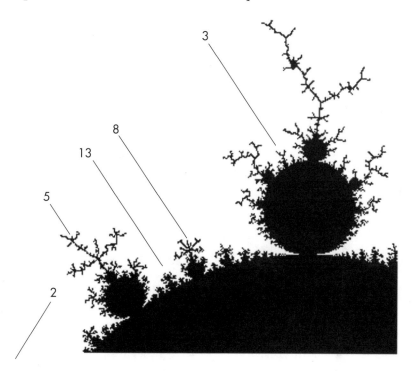

The sequence of bulbs associated with the Fibonacci sequence gets smaller and smaller and tends to a point on the boundary of the main cardioid. This point does not correspond to a bulb but rather, to a single c-value. The nature of the orbits for this special c-value was a major unanswered question in mathematics for decades.

IRRATIONAL NUMBERS

We have seen that there is a bulb corresponding to each fraction (in lowest terms) between 0 and 1. The natural question is: What about the irrational numbers? Well, they are there, but they do not appear as bulbs. For example, in the Fibonacci sequence above, there is a sequence of smaller and smaller bulbs corresponding to the entries in the sequence, and these bulbs converge to a single point on the boundary of the main cardioid. This point then corresponds to an irrational closely related to "the golden ratio," one of the most famous irrationals. In fact, all sequences of converging rational numbers constructed in this way converge to points on the boundary of the main cardioid corresponding to irrational numbers.

Now we understand the filled Julia sets and the fate of orbits for some of these irrationals, but not for all of them. In particular, thanks to the work of the French mathematician Jean-Christophe Yoccoz (1957), we understand completely the irrationals that are "highly irrational" or "far from rationals." We still do not understand what is happening to the irrationals that are "close to rational numbers." Unfortunately, we don't have time or space to tell you what being "far from rationals" means.

Yoccoz's work is one of the major achievements in this field of mathematics in recent years. For this work, he was awarded the Fields Medal (the equivalent of the Nobel Prize in mathematics) in 1994. See

http://www-groups.dcs.st-andrews.ac.uk/~history/Mathematicians/Yoccoz.html

With a little perseverance and more work (well, maybe a lot more work), you can help to figure out the remaining mysteries of the Mandelbrot set.

BEYOND THE MANDELBROT SET

Another question that often arises is: What about other iteration rules? Is there an analogue of the Mandelbrot set for these rules?

Certain other rules have been investigated in detail. For example, the family of iterations of the form $x \to x^n + c$ can be handled just like the quadratic iteration because 0 is also the critical orbit for this family. But if we take a more general polynomial, say, $x \to x^3 + Ax + B$, then we are in trouble. The graph of $y = x^3 + Ax + B$ often has two critical points: a maximum and a minimum. To paint the picture of the analogue of the Mandelbrot set, we will have to follow two critical orbits, not just one. Equivalently, this family depends on two complex parameters A and B, not just one as in the case of $x \to x^2 + c$. This means that the analogue of the Mandelbrot set will lie in AB-space, which is a four-dimensional space (since both A and B are complex numbers). Think of how hard it was to comprehend the two-dimensional Mandelbrot set, and then try to imagine the difficulties four dimensions would present. It is little wonder that we are far, very far, from understanding these more complicated iteration rules.

WHAT ARE THE APPLICATIONS OF THIS MATHEMATICS?

The easy answer to this question is that there are none. The fact is that we still do not understand completely all of the mathematics behind the Mandelbrot set, so we cannot begin to apply the mathematics to other situations. This is often the case in mathematics. The mathematical ideas usually have to be completely developed in order for them to be applied. Sometimes it takes years or even centuries before certain mathematical ideas find their role in applications but, inevitably, the mathematics proves useful.

This doesn't mean that the Mandelbrot set has no applications. As we saw much earlier, ecologists often are interested in iteration rules such as the logistic rule, a slightly different quadratic iteration. As we also saw, this real iteration is very complicated. What mathematicians do in this case is to make the problem seemingly harder by considering the complex iteration instead. However, when we look at the iteration rule from a more general perspective, we begin to see structures (like the Mandelbrot set) that have some patterns within. Once we see and understand these patterns, we can go back to the original problem and, hopefully, make some progress.

There is another arena where the Mandelbrot set shows up. In many applications, it is important to be able to solve equations. Unfortunately, most equations cannot be solved by hand (sadly, there is no general-purpose equation solver like the quadratic formula that works for all equations). So, whenever a scientist or an engineer confronts an equation that must be solved, he or she turns to the computer, much as we did in the book *Iteration* in this series, to find square roots. The computer then invokes some numerical scheme, usually an iterative process, to solve the equation approximately. Unfortunately, these numerical procedures do not always work, so it is important for the scientist or engineer to know when the computer is producing erroneous results. The typical procedure is to ask the computer to plot the parameter values where the algorithm involved is not working properly. When the computer does this, the picture that often results is—you guessed it—the Mandelbrot set. So, in the midst of an important calculation, when we ask, "Is this algorithm working properly?" we often have to confront the Mandelbrot set as the set of "bad" parameters for our problem.

1 ▷ FIND THE ROTATION NUMBERS

By eye, determine the rotation numbers corresponding to each of the following filled Julia sets. Then compute the corresponding cycle to which the orbit of 0 tends. Indicate this cycle on the filled Julia set using x_0, x_1, x_2, ... Does the cycle move around the ears as you expected?

a. $c = -0.62 - 0.43i$

b. $c = 0.28 + 0.53i$

c. $c = -0.62 + 0.42i$

d. $c = -1 + 0.2i$

e. $c = -0.36 + 0.62i$

f. $c = 0.38 - 0.34i$

THE MANDELBROT AND JULIA SETS: A TOOL KIT OF DYNAMICS ACTIVITIES
©2000 KEY CURRICULUM PRESS

2 ▷ ROTATION NUMBERS AND BULBS

Using the rotation numbers found in Investigation 1, identify the corresponding six bulbs in this Mandelbrot set:

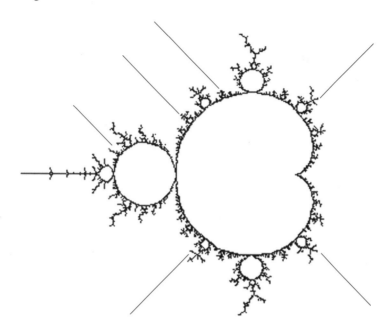

3 ▷ MORE BULBS AND ROTATION NUMBERS

Identify the rotation number corresponding to each of these bulbs in the Mandelbrot set:

a.

b.

c. _____

d. _____

e. _____

f. _____

g. _____

4 ▷ FIND THE CORRESPONDING BULBS

Each of the bulbs in Investigation 3 came from the area of the Mandelbrot set pictured below. Using software that allows you to magnify portions of the Mandelbrot set, identify the corresponding bulbs and rotation numbers. The Mandelbrot Set Explorer at **http://math.bu.edu/DYSYS/explorer** will be helpful.

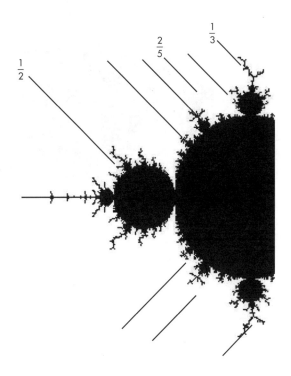

5 ▷ IDENTIFY THE BULBS

For each bulb hanging directly off the main cardioid, we may determine the
rotation number using any of the methods previously discussed. Fill in the
following diagram with the appropriate rotation numbers.

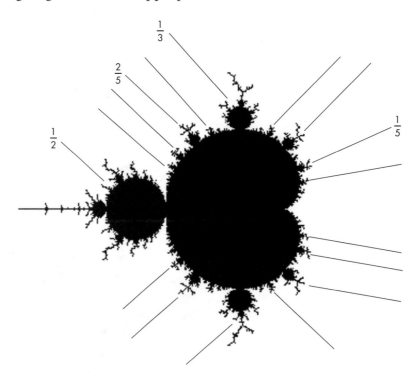

6 ▷ ORDER THE BULBS

Look at how the rotation numbers are arranged around the cardioid in
Investigation 5. What pattern do you see?

_____

_____

_____

_____

Check your conjecture by choosing several other bulbs and seeing if the bulbs
are still arranged in the same order.

7 ▷ THE LARGEST BULBS IN BETWEEN

a. What is the rotation number corresponding to the largest bulb between the
¹/₃- and ¹/₄-bulbs? _____

b. Between the ¹/₃- and ²/₅-bulbs? _____

c. Between the ²/₅- and ³/₇-bulbs? _____

Now you must promise never to add fractions that way again, OK? Sign here:

8 ▷ THE ½-BULB

Here is a magnification of the period-2 bulb in the Mandelbrot set. Using a computer, determine the period of each of the indicated bulbs directly attached to this bulb. Use the Mandelbrot Set Explorer at **http://math.bu.edu/DYSYS/explorer.**

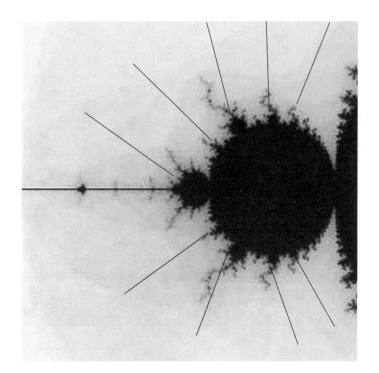

What is the pattern of how these bulbs are arranged?

_____

_____

_____

9 ▷ THE ⅓-BULB

Here is the ⅓-bulb. Determine the period of each of the smaller bulbs (the secondary bulbs) directly attached to this bulb. The Mandelbrot Set Explorer at **http://math.bu.edu/DYSYS/explorer** will help.

What is the pattern of how these bulbs are arranged?

_____

_____

_____

Answers

LESSON 1 ▷ QUADRATIC ITERATION

INVESTIGATION 1: FATES OF ORBITS

$c = 0.3$: Orbit of 0 tends to infinity.

$c = 0.2$: Tends to a fixed point at $0.276 \ldots$

$c = 0.0$: 0 is a fixed point

$c = -0.5$: Tends to a fixed point at -0.366

$c = -1.1$: Tends to a 2-cycle at $-1.09 \ldots, 0.09 \ldots$

$c = -1.3$: Tends to a 4-cycle at $0.019 \ldots, -1.299 \ldots, 0.389 \ldots, -1.149 \ldots$

$c = -1.38$: Tends to an 8-cycle

$c = -1.6$: Apparently chaotic

$c = -1.76$: Tends to a 3-cycle at $-1.759 \ldots, 1.335 \ldots, 0.024 \ldots$

$c = -1.77$: Tends to a 6-cycle

$c = -1.8$: Apparently chaotic (We say "apparently chaotic" because the orbit could in fact lie on a cycle of *very* long period, although numerical error would never allow us to see this exactly.)

INVESTIGATION 2: GRAPHICAL ITERATION

Here is the fate of the orbit of 0 (it tends
to a 4-cycle):

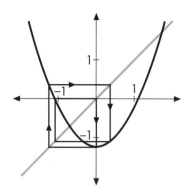

INVESTIGATION 3: ESCAPING ORBITS

a. There are exactly two intervals of
points whose orbits leave the box at
the second iteration. One way to see
this is through graphical iteration:
Orbits that start in the interior of the
intervals marked *A* and *B* are sent
after one iteration to the original
exit set. So these orbits leave after
two iterations.

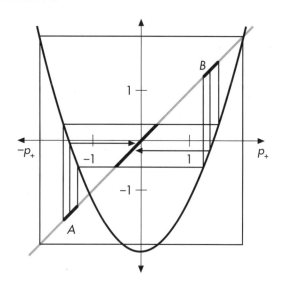

b. There are four intervals containing
points whose orbits exit after three
iterations. They are marked *C–F*
below. Note that they contain points
whose orbits enter either *A* or *B* after
one iteration.

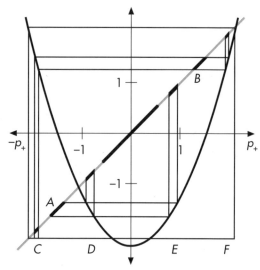

c. There are then eight intervals whose orbits enter C–F at the next iteration. Continuing, there are 2^n intervals whose orbits leave at exactly iteration number n. There is another way to see this: We can simply graph the higher iterations of $x^2 + c$ and see where these graphs poke out of the box.

INVESTIGATION 4: TYPES OF FIXED POINTS

a. The fixed points marked A and B are repelling; the fixed point at 0 is attracting.

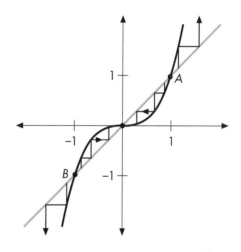

b. The fixed point marked A is attracting; the fixed point at 0 is neutral.

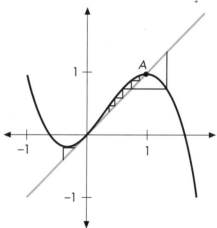

INVESTIGATION 5: FINDING CYCLES GRAPHICALLY

The graph of F shows that this iteration rule has two fixed points:

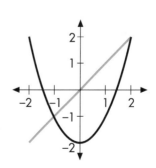

The graph of $y = F^2(x)$ crosses the diagonal four times. Two of these crossings must be the previous fixed points; the other two are new. So these must be a 2-cycle.

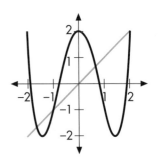

The graph of $y = F^3(x)$ crosses the diagonal eight times. Two of these crossings are fixed points. None can be the 2-cycle above, since these points are fixed only by even iterations. So the remaining six points have to lie on 3-cycles.

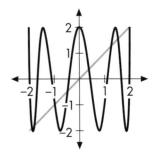

So we have two fixed points, two points lying on a 2-cycle, and six points lying on a 3-cycle.

INVESTIGATION 6: FINDING CYCLES ALGEBRAICALLY

To find 2-cycles, we must first iterate twice $x \to x^2 + c \to (x^2 + c)^2 + c$ and then solve the equation $(x^2 + c)^2 + c = x$. This amounts to finding the roots of the fourth-degree equation $x^4 + 2cx^2 - x + c^2 + c = 0$. Now we know that two of these roots are the fixed points, which are given by the roots of $x^2 + c = x$, or $x^2 - x + c = 0$. So we can divide the preceding fourth-degree polynomial by this quadratic polynomial to find

$$\frac{x^4 + 2cx^2 - x + c^2 + c}{x^2 - x + c} = x^2 + x + (c + 1)$$

So the 2-cycles must be solutions of the quadratic equation $x^2 + x + (c + 1) = 0$. By the quadratic formula, these roots are

$$q_\pm = \frac{-1 \pm \sqrt{1 - 4(c + 1)}}{2} \quad \text{or} \quad q_\pm = \frac{-1 \pm \sqrt{-3 - 4c}}{2}$$

There is a 2-cycle if $c \leq -3/4$. Actually, when $c = -3/4$, both points on the 2-cycle merge and we have a fixed point $q_+ = q_- = -1/2$.

LESSON 2: ▷ COMPLEX LINEAR ITERATION

INVESTIGATION 1: REVIEW OF POLAR REPRESENTATIONS

a. $r = 4, \theta = -90°$ or $-\pi/2$ radians

b. $r = \sqrt{2}, \theta = -45°$ or $-\pi/4$ radians $\frac{-1}{\sqrt{2}} + \frac{i}{\sqrt{2}}$

c. $r = \sqrt{8} = 2\sqrt{2}, \theta = 45°$ or $\pi/4$ radians

d. $r = 6, \theta = 0°$ or 0 radians

e. $r = \sqrt{8} = 2\sqrt{2}, \theta = -135°$ or $-3\pi/4$ radians

f. $r = 15, \theta = 180° = -180°$ or π radians $= -\pi$ radians

INVESTIGATION 2: REVIEW OF COMPLEX GEOMETRY

a. -4

b. $\sqrt{2} + \sqrt{2}i$

c. $\frac{-1}{\sqrt{2}} + \frac{i}{\sqrt{2}}$

d. $-3.23i$

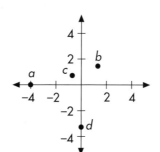

INVESTIGATION 3: REVIEW OF COMPLEX ARITHMETIC

a. $5 + 10i$

b. $-8 + 12i$

c. $14 + 8i$

d. $-64 + 112i$

INVESTIGATION 4: COMPLEX LINEAR ITERATION RULES

a. Orbit: $0 \to i \to 2i \to 3i \to 4i \to \cdots$ This orbit goes to infinity along the imaginary axis.

b. Orbit: $16 - 16i \to 8 - 8i \to 4 - 4i \to 2 - 2i \to 1 - i \to$
$0.5 - 0.5i \to 0.25 - 0.25i \to 1/8 - i/8 \to 1/16 - i/16 \to \cdots$ The orbit tends to 0.

c. Orbit: $0 \to -i \to 0 \to -i \to 0 \to \cdots$ The orbit is a 2-cycle.

d. Orbit: $1 + i \to -1 + i \to -1 - i \to 1 - i \to 1 + i \to \cdots$ The orbit is a 4-cycle.

e. Orbit: $i \to 0 \to 1 \to 1 + i \to i \to \cdots$ The orbit is a 4-cycle.

INVESTIGATION 5: PLOTTING ORBITS IN THE COMPLEX PLANE

a.

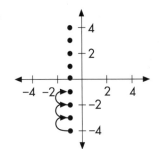

b.

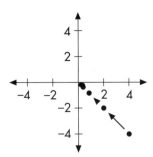

c.

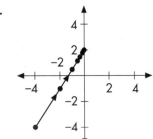

d.

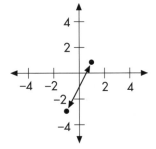

e.

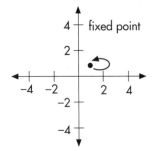

f.

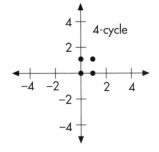

INVESTIGATION 6: LINEAR ITERATION RULES

a. All nonzero orbits lie on a 4-cycle.

b. Trick question! The iteration rule is just $x \to ix$, same as in part a.

c. All nonzero orbits lie on a 3-cycle, since each time we multiply, we simply rotate by $2\pi/3$ radians or 120°. For example, the orbit of 1 is

$$1 \to \cos\frac{2\pi}{3} + i\sin\frac{2\pi}{3} \to \cos\frac{4\pi}{3} + i\sin\frac{4\pi}{3} \to 1 \to \cdots$$

d. All nonzero orbits lie on a 5-cycle, since each time we multiply, we simply rotate by $2\pi/5$ radians or 72°.

e. All nonzero orbits lie on a 79-cycle, since each time we multiply, we simply rotate by $2\pi/79$ radians or $\left(360/79\right)^\circ$.

f. Since any number whose magnitude is 1 must lie on the circle of radius 1 centered at the origin, we can write such a number in the form $\cos(2\pi\theta) + i\sin(2\pi\theta)$. That is, if the magnitude of $a + bi$ is 1, the iteration rule $x \to (a + bi)x$ can be written as $x \to \left(\cos(2\pi\theta) + i\sin(2\pi\theta)\right)x$.

This means that each time we multiply by $\cos(2\pi\theta) + i\sin(2\pi\theta)$, we simply rotate the point on a circle centered at the origin by $2\pi\theta$ radians in the counterclockwise direction. If $\theta = 1/2$, we rotate each point halfway around the circle. Therefore, after two iterations we return to our original position, so all nonzero points lie on 2-cycles. Of course, when $\theta = 1/2$, $\cos(2\pi\theta) + i\sin(2\pi\theta) = \cos(\pi) + i\sin(\pi) = -1$, so we are really using the iteration rule $x \to -x$. It is no surprise that all points have period 2 for this rule.

If $\theta = 1/3$, then each point is rotated one-third of the way around the circle in the counterclockwise direction. So all points have period 3 in this case. In general, if $\theta = p/q$ (with p/q in lowest terms), we rotate points an angular distance of p/q turns around the circle (that is, by $2\pi p/q$ radians) at each iteration. Therefore, all orbits lie on a q-cycle.

When θ is an irrational number, there are no cycles. In fact, each orbit winds around a circle of given magnitude without ever coming back to its original point. The reason for this is, after n iterations, we have rotated each point by $2\pi n\theta$ radians. If an orbit were to come back to its seed after n iterations, we would need $2\pi n\theta$ to be an integer multiple of 2π. That is, we would have $2\pi n\theta = \text{integer} \cdot 2\pi$. But then we would have $\theta = \text{integer}/n$, contradicting the fact that θ was irrational.

INVESTIGATION 7: ROTATIONS

a. All nonzero orbits rotate by $^2/_5$ of a turn around the origin ($144°$ or $^{4\pi}/_5$ radians).

b. All nonzero orbits rotate by $^3/_7$ of a turn around the origin.

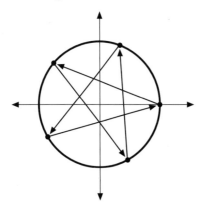 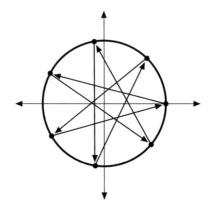

c. Each nonzero orbit features 71 points equally spaced on a circle about the origin. Points are rotated counterclockwise by $^1/_{71}$ of a turn at each iteration.

d. Each nonzero orbit features q points equally spaced on a circle about the origin. Points are rotated counterclockwise by $^p/_q$ of a turn at each iteration. Here is the picture for $\theta = ^1/_7$:

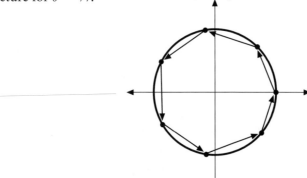

and for $\theta = ^2/_7$:

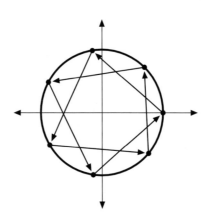

INVESTIGATION 8: GENERAL LINEAR ITERATION RULES

a. The fixed points for the iteration rule $x \rightarrow Ax + B$ are given by solving $Ax + B = x$. This yields $x = {}^{-B}\!/_{(A-1)}$.

b. If $A = 1$, the preceding formula has problems. If B is nonzero, then we have no fixed points. Orbits are of the form $x \rightarrow x + B \rightarrow x + 2B \rightarrow x + 3B \rightarrow \cdots$. If $B = 0$, then our iteration rule is $x \rightarrow x$ for which all points are fixed points.

c. From part b, only when $A = 1$, $B = 0$ do we have more than one fixed point.

d. When A does not equal 1, there is a unique fixed point.

LESSON 3: ▷ THE SQUARING RULE

INVESTIGATION 1: ORBITS UNDER COMPLEX SQUARING

a. $-1 \rightarrow 1 \rightarrow 1 \rightarrow \cdots$ Eventually fixed

b. $2i \rightarrow -4 \rightarrow 16 \rightarrow 256 \rightarrow \cdots$ Goes to infinity

c. $\frac{1}{2}i \rightarrow -\frac{1}{4} \rightarrow \frac{1}{16} \rightarrow \frac{1}{256} \cdots$ Goes to 0

d. $1 + i \rightarrow 2i \rightarrow -4 \rightarrow 16 \rightarrow 256 \rightarrow \cdots$ Goes to infinity

e. $\frac{1}{\sqrt{2}} + \frac{1}{\sqrt{2}}i \rightarrow i \rightarrow -1 \rightarrow 1 \rightarrow 1 \rightarrow \cdots$ Eventually fixed

f. $\frac{1 + \sqrt{3}i}{2} \rightarrow \frac{-1 + \sqrt{3}i}{2} \rightarrow \frac{-1 - \sqrt{3}i}{2} \rightarrow \frac{-1 + \sqrt{3}i}{2} \rightarrow \frac{-1 - \sqrt{3}i}{2} \rightarrow \cdots$ Eventual 2-cycle

INVESTIGATION 2: PLOTTING ORBITS

a. Orbit goes to 0.　　**b.** Orbit goes to infinity.　　**c.** Orbit cycles with period 2.

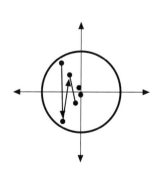 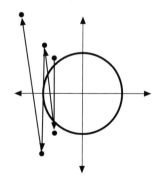 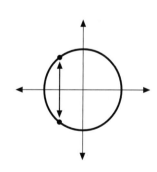

d. Orbit goes to infinity.

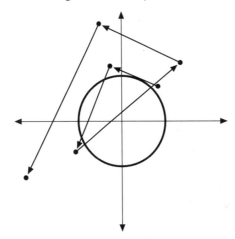

e. Orbit goes to 0.

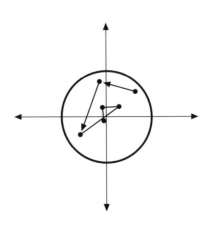

INVESTIGATION 3: THREE SEEDS IN THE COMPLEX PLANE

All locations shown are only approximate: The goal is simply to double the polar angle and square the magnitude.

A.

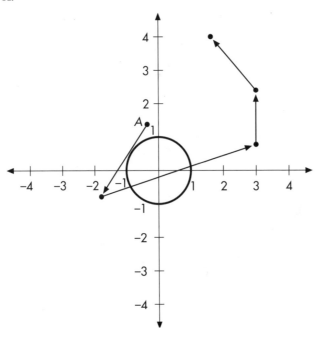

B.

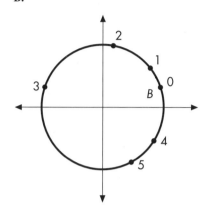

C.

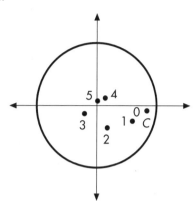

INVESTIGATION 4: ORBITS ON THE UNIT CIRCLE

a. $\frac{1}{7} \to \frac{2}{7} \to \frac{4}{7} \to \frac{1}{7} \to \cdots$ 3-cycle

b. $\frac{1}{9} \to \frac{2}{9} \to \frac{4}{9} \to \frac{8}{9} \to \frac{7}{9} \to \frac{5}{9} \to \frac{1}{9} \to \cdots$ 6-cycle

c. $\frac{1}{5} \to \frac{2}{5} \to \frac{4}{5} \to \frac{3}{5} \to \frac{1}{5} \to \cdots$ 4-cycle

d. $\frac{3}{28} \to \frac{3}{14} \to \frac{3}{7} \to \frac{6}{7} \to \frac{5}{7} \to \frac{3}{7} \to \cdots$ Eventual 3-cycle

e. $\frac{1}{16} \to \frac{1}{8} \to \frac{1}{4} \to \frac{1}{2} \to 0 \to 0 \to \cdots$ Eventually fixed (Note that 0 is the same as 1 in terms of revolutions.)

f. $\frac{5}{11} \to \frac{10}{11} \to \frac{9}{11} \to \frac{7}{11} \to \frac{3}{11} \to \frac{6}{11} \to \frac{1}{11} \to \frac{2}{11} \to \frac{4}{11} \to \frac{8}{11} \to \frac{5}{11} \to \cdots$ 10-cycle

g. $\frac{7}{24} \to \frac{7}{12} \to \frac{1}{6} \to \frac{1}{3} \to \frac{2}{3} \to \frac{1}{3} \to \cdots$ Eventual 2-cycle

INVESTIGATION 5: ORBITS UNDER DOUBLING

a. If q is odd, the orbit lies on a cycle. If q is even, the orbit lies on an eventual cycle. If q is odd, each time we "double" the number of revolutions, we never cancel a 2 from the denominator. So the orbit of $\frac{p}{q}$ consists of fractions in which each denominator is q. Now suppose we have two fractions $\frac{a}{q}$ and $\frac{b}{q}$ with q odd and $0 \le a, b < q$. Suppose we double each of them and end up with the same number of revolutions. This means that $\frac{2a}{q} = \frac{2b}{q} + 1$ or $2a = 2b + q$. But the left side here is even, while the right is odd, so this cannot have happened. This means that doubling simply permutes all the fractions of the form $\frac{a}{q}$ when q is odd, so we must return to $\frac{a}{q}$ after a finite number of doublings. That is, $\frac{a}{q}$ lies on a cycle.

b. When q is even, each time we double we can factor out a 2 from the denominator until the denominator is odd. This means that the orbit eventually meets a fraction with an odd denominator and so eventually cycles.

INVESTIGATION 6: FINDING CYCLES

Fixed point: Only 0 revolutions.

Period 2: $\frac{1}{3} \rightarrow \frac{2}{3} \rightarrow \cdots$

Period 3: $\frac{1}{7} \rightarrow \frac{2}{7} \rightarrow \frac{4}{7} \rightarrow \frac{1}{7} \rightarrow \cdots$ and $\frac{3}{7} \rightarrow \frac{6}{7} \rightarrow \frac{5}{7} \rightarrow \frac{3}{7} \rightarrow \cdots$

Period 4: $\frac{1}{15} \rightarrow \frac{2}{15} \rightarrow \frac{4}{15} \rightarrow \frac{8}{15} \rightarrow \frac{1}{15} \rightarrow \cdots$
$\frac{7}{15} \rightarrow \frac{14}{15} \rightarrow \frac{13}{15} \rightarrow \frac{11}{15} \rightarrow \frac{7}{15} \rightarrow \cdots$
$\frac{3}{15} \rightarrow \frac{6}{15} \rightarrow \frac{12}{15} \rightarrow \frac{9}{15} \rightarrow \frac{3}{15} \rightarrow \cdots$ (More commonly the orbit of $\frac{1}{5}$, but we write it this way to see the pattern.) Note that $\frac{5}{15} \rightarrow \frac{10}{15} \rightarrow \frac{5}{15} \rightarrow \cdots$ has period 2.

Period 5: The orbits of $\frac{1}{31}$, $\frac{3}{31}$, $\frac{5}{31}$, $\frac{7}{31}$, and $\frac{11}{31}$ all are distinct and have period 5.

Period 6: Fractions of the form $\frac{p}{63}$ ($p > 0$) have period 6, except those with lower periods, namely, those of the form $\frac{q}{7}$, which have period 3.

The wonderful fact is that any fraction whose denominator is $2^q - 1$ is periodic with a period that divides q.

INVESTIGATION 7: SENSITIVITY TO INITIAL CONDITIONS

It is precisely the seeds that lie on the unit circle (the Julia set) that exhibit sensitive dependence to initial conditions, for arbitrarily close to any such seed is a point whose orbit tends to 0 and another whose orbit tends to infinity. Meanwhile, the chosen seed has an orbit that remains for all iterations on the unit circle.

Inside the unit circle, all orbits behave the same way: They tend to 0. Outside, orbits also behave similarly: They go to infinity. In the latter case, it is true that the distance between these orbits grows, but the fact is that all of these orbits do share the same fate.

LESSON 4: ▷ JULIA SETS OF QUADRATIC ITERATIONS

INVESTIGATION 1: COMPUTING ORBITS

a. $x_0 = 1$ Orbit is eventually periodic with period 2, so it is in the filled Julia set.

b. $x_0 = 0.2 - 0.2i$ Orbit tends to the 2-cycle $0 \rightarrow -1 \rightarrow 0 \rightarrow \cdots$, so it is in the filled Julia set.

c. $x_0 = -1 + 0.1i$ Orbit tends to the 2-cycle $0 \rightarrow -1 \rightarrow 0 \rightarrow \cdots$, so it is in the filled Julia set.

d. $x_0 = -1 + 0.4i$ Orbit tends to infinity. Not in the filled Julia set.

INVESTIGATION 2: COMPUTING FILLED JULIA SETS

All three of these computations should yield more or less the same image. There may be a difference of a pixel or two here and there, but basically the result should resemble this:

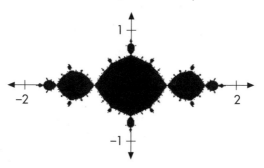

In terms of self-similarity, this filled Julia set basically consists of disks attached to disks attached to disks. Everywhere you look you see two disks attached at a single junction point. Here is a magnification of the "top" of this filled Julia set:

Magnifying a portion of the "northeast" side of this image yields this:

As you see, the basic shape remains the same: disk attached to disk attached to disk and so on.

INVESTIGATION 3: MATCHING FILLED JULIA SETS

a. III   b. IV   c. I   d. II

e. VIII   f. VII   g. V   h. VI

INVESTIGATION 4: FATE OF THE CRITICAL ORBIT

a. Tends to a 2-cycle.

b. Tends to a 5-cycle.

c. Tends to a 5-cycle.

d. Tends to a fixed point.

e. Tends to a 7-cycle.

f. Tends to a fixed point.

g. Tends to a 6-cycle.

h. Tends to a 7-cycle.

Note that if the orbit of 0 tends to a k-cycle, then the filled Julia set features junction points which, when removed, leave exactly k disjoint pieces. In the case of a fixed point, there are no junction points, so the filled Julia set is just one piece.

It is important to realize that we have chosen very special filled Julia sets here. As we will see in the next lesson, these are Julia sets that come from the principal bulb of the Mandelbrot set. When c-values are chosen from other regions of the Mandelbrot set, different geometries apply. For example, here is a filled Julia set corresponding to a cycle of period 6. Looking closely at this filled Julia set, it appears that we have replaced the fractal rabbit's belly and ears with filled Julia sets that look like period-2 sets as in Investigation 2. We have actually chosen a c-value from the period-6 bulb hanging off the principal period-3 bulb.

INVESTIGATION 5: FRACTAL DUST OR CONNECTED?

a. $x \rightarrow x^2 - 0.1 - 0.75i$

b. $x \rightarrow x^2 + 0.12 - 0.75i$

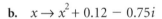

Critical orbit tends to a 3-cycle.
Filled Julia set is connected.

Critical orbit tends to infinity.
Filled Julia set is fractal dust.

c. $x \rightarrow x^2 + 0.286 + 0.54i$

Critical orbit tends to a 4-cycle.
Filled Julia set is connected.

d. $x \rightarrow x^2 + 0.486 + 0.54i$

Critical orbit tends to infinity.
Filled Julia set is fractal dust.

e. $x \rightarrow x^2 - 0.6 - 0.55i$

Critical orbit tends to infinity.
Filled Julia set is fractal dust.

f. $x \rightarrow x^2 - 0.5 - 0.55i$

Critical orbit tends to a 5-cycle.
Filled Julia set is connected.

g. $x \rightarrow x^2 + 0.451 + 0.216i$

Critical orbit tends to infinity.
Filled Julia set is fractal dust.

h. $x \rightarrow x^2 + 0.392 + 0.216i$

Critical orbit tends to a 6-cycle.
Filled Julia set is connected.

i. $x \rightarrow x^2 - 0.624 - 0.441i$

Critical orbit tends to a 7-cycle.
Filled Julia set is connected.

j. $x \rightarrow x^2 - 0.23 + 0.45i$

Critical orbit tends to a fixed point.
Filled Julia set is connected.

INVESTIGATION 6: THE FUNDAMENTAL DICHOTOMY

It appears that the filled Julia set is fractal dust whenever the critical orbit escapes, while the filled Julia set is connected when the critical orbit does not escape. This is indeed the case, though the proof of this theorem demands much more advanced mathematics, namely, complex analysis. So this is the fundamental dichotomy: There are only two "types" of filled Julia sets, connected sets and fractal dust. There is nothing in between, such as a filled Julia set that consists of 5 or 50 or 500 pieces; only 1 or infinitely many pieces are allowed. Even more amazing is the fact that it is the orbit of 0 that determines which of these two possibilities occurs. We will explore this fact in the next lesson when we consider the Mandelbrot set.

INVESTIGATION 7: THE c-PLANE

Here is a plot of the ten c-values from Investigation 5:

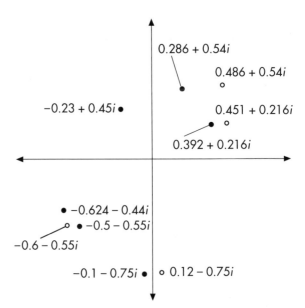

Now here is a plot of the Mandelbrot set with the same ten c-values superimposed. We will cover this story in the next lesson in detail. All chosen c-values for which the critical orbit escapes should lie outside the Mandelbrot set.

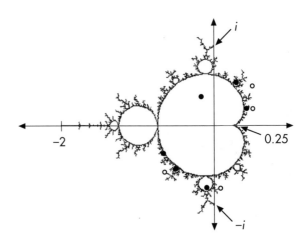

LESSON 5: ▷ THE MANDELBROT SET

INVESTIGATION 1: LOCATING *c*-VALUES

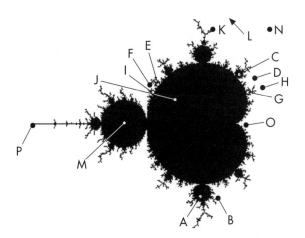

a. In *M*: Orbit of 0 tends to a 3-cycle.

b. Not in *M*: Orbit of 0 escapes.

c. In *M*: Orbit of 0 tends to a 4-cycle.

d. Not in *M*: Orbit of 0 escapes.

e. In *M*: Orbit of 0 tends to a 5-cycle.

f. Not in *M*: Orbit of 0 escapes.

g. In *M*: Orbit of 0 tends to a 5-cycle.

h. Not in *M*: Orbit of 0 escapes.

i. In *M*: Orbit of 0 tends to a 7-cycle.

j. In *M*: Orbit of 0 tends to a fixed point.

k. In *M*: Orbit of 0 is eventually a 2-cycle. You can compute this orbit exactly:

$$0 \to i \to -1 + i \to -i \to -1 + i \to \cdots$$

With a computer, however, it usually appears that the orbit escapes. You have to be very careful sometimes!

l. Not in *M*: Orbit of 0 escapes.

m. In *M*: Orbit of 0 tends to a 4-cycle.

n. Not in *M*: Orbit of 0 escapes.

o. Not in *M*: Orbit of 0 escapes.

p. In *M*: Orbit of 0 is eventually fixed:

$$0 \to -2 \to 2 \to 2 \to \cdots$$

INVESTIGATION 2: THE MAIN CARDIOID

c. For each *c*-value inside the main cardioid, the filled
Julia set is surrounded by a simple curve as in this picture:

The curve could be the unit circle, as in the case $c = 0$.
Most often, it is a fractal curve because it consists of
infinitely many jagged corners everywhere. In practice,
this fractal nature is very difficult to see. The main point
is that the boundary of the filled Julia set has no junction
points as in the case of filled Julia sets drawn from other
areas of the Mandelbrot set. In each case, the orbit tends
to a fixed point.

INVESTIGATION 3: THE PERIOD-3 BULB

The fate of the orbit of 0 is always the same: It tends to a 3-cycle. A word of warning
here: By the period-3 bulb, we mean only the largest visible disk, not the smaller disks
or decorations hanging off this bulb. These have different periods, as we will see later.

INVESTIGATION 4: PERIOD-*k* BULBS

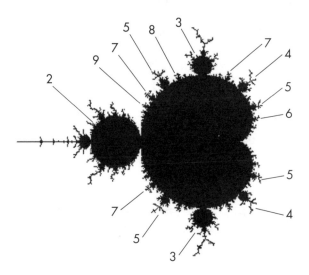

INVESTIGATION 5: SYMMETRY IN THE MANDELBROT SET

The Mandelbrot set is symmetric about the real axis. Moreover, the periods of
symmetrically located bulbs are the same.

INVESTIGATION 6: GEOMETRY OF THE BULBS

It appears that the number of spokes emanating from the junction point of the antenna (counting the principal spoke) is the same as the period of the bulb.

   a. 7   **b.** 4   **c.** 5

   d. 12   **e.** 12   **f.** 7

INVESTIGATION 7: FILLED JULIA SETS AND PERIODS OF BULBS

It appears that the number of pieces of filled Julia set that remain after removing a junction point is the same as the period.

   a. 4   **b.** 7   **c.** 3

   d. 2   **e.** 5   **f.** 5

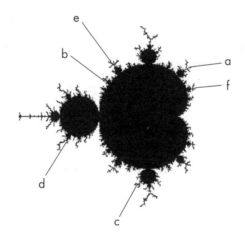

LESSON 6: ▷ GEOMETRY OF THE MANDELBROT SET

INVESTIGATION 1: FIND THE ROTATION NUMBERS

   a. Rotation number $\frac{3}{5}$:   **b.** Rotation number $\frac{1}{4}$:

c. Rotation number $\frac{3}{7}$:

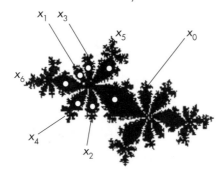

d. Rotation number $\frac{1}{2}$:

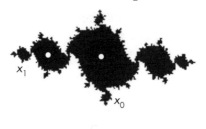

e. Rotation number $\frac{3}{8}$:

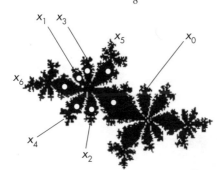

f. Rotation number $\frac{4}{5}$:

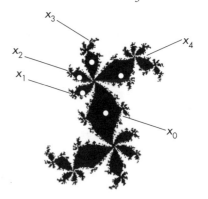

INVESTIGATION 2: ROTATION NUMBERS AND BULBS

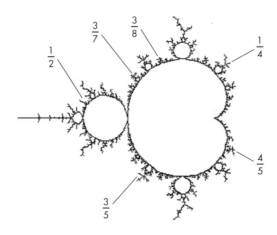

INVESTIGATION 3: MORE BULBS AND ROTATION NUMBERS

a. $\frac{3}{5}$

b. $\frac{4}{7}$

c. $\frac{5}{12}$

d. $\frac{2}{3}$

e. $\frac{3}{8}$

f. $\frac{4}{9}$

g. $\frac{6}{13}$

INVESTIGATION 4: FIND THE CORRESPONDING BULBS

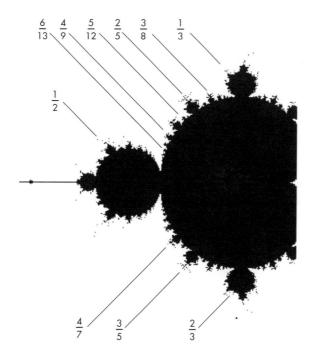

INVESTIGATION 5: IDENTIFY THE BULBS

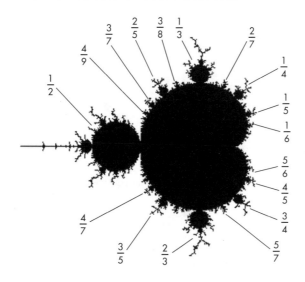

INVESTIGATION 6: ORDER THE BULBS

The bulbs hanging off the main cardioid are arranged in the exact order of the rational numbers (the fractions), beginning at 0, which can be interpreted as the cusp of the main cardioid, and then proceeding counterclockwise through each fraction until returning to the cusp at 1.

INVESTIGATION 7: THE LARGEST BULBS IN BETWEEN

a.–c. The largest bulb between the $\frac{1}{3}$- and $\frac{1}{4}$-bulbs is the $\frac{2}{7}$-bulb. The largest bulb between the $\frac{1}{3}$- and $\frac{2}{5}$-bulbs is the $\frac{3}{8}$-bulb. The largest bulb between the $\frac{2}{5}$- and $\frac{3}{7}$-bulbs is the $\frac{5}{12}$-bulb.

There is a beautiful mathematical story unfolding here. From elementary number theory, you can write, in a tree-like structure, the fraction between two given fractions in the tree that has the smallest denominator. Begin with 0 and 1, which we choose to write as $\frac{0}{1}$ and $\frac{1}{1}$ for reasons that will become apparent in a moment. So, at this initial stage, the tree is

$$\frac{0}{1} \qquad\qquad\qquad\qquad\qquad \frac{1}{1}$$

The fraction between $\frac{0}{1}$ and $\frac{1}{1}$ that has the smallest denominator is $\frac{1}{2}$, so we insert this between the two "parents":

$$\frac{0}{1} \qquad\qquad \frac{1}{2} \qquad\qquad \frac{1}{1}$$

Note that this fraction is obtained by adding the numerators and denominators of the "parents."

Now we continue in the same fashion. The fraction between $\frac{0}{1}$ and $\frac{1}{2}$ with the lowest denominator is $\frac{1}{3}$; the fraction between $\frac{1}{2}$ and $\frac{1}{1}$ with the lowest denominator is $\frac{2}{3}$. Again, these fractions are obtained by the curious addition rule. The next stage of the tree is

$$\frac{0}{1} \qquad \frac{1}{3} \qquad \frac{1}{2} \qquad \frac{2}{3} \qquad \frac{1}{1}$$

Continuing:

$$\frac{0}{1} \quad \frac{1}{4} \quad \frac{1}{3} \quad \frac{2}{5} \quad \frac{1}{2} \quad \frac{3}{5} \quad \frac{2}{3} \quad \frac{3}{4} \quad \frac{1}{1}$$

Again we see that the smallest fraction between two given "parents" is obtained by adding the denominators and numerators. This fact has been known since the beginning of the nineteenth century. The tree is called the "Farey tree" and the curious method of addition is called "Farey addition," after its inventor, John Farey (1766–1826), an English civil engineer and mathematician.

INVESTIGATION 8: THE ½-BULB

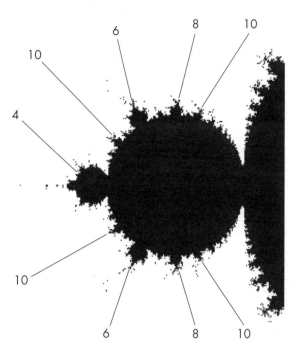

These bulbs are arranged in the exact same order as the bulbs hanging off the main cardioid, except their periods are doubled.

INVESTIGATION 9: THE ⅓-BULB

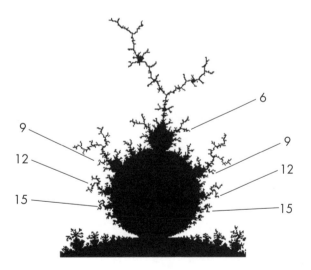

As in the previous Investigation, these bulbs are arranged in the exact same order as the bulbs hanging off the main cardioid, except their periods are tripled. This is in fact true about any bulb. The "baby bulbs" hanging off a period-n bulb have periods n times the periods hanging off the main cardioid and are arranged in the same order.